Praise for the *Warrior*

"The *Warrior Mum Blog* is a tangible and powerful storie... sincere women who have so ... ...derstand. Often we as Learnir... ...are seen as the specialists and yet we have so ...uch to learn from others who are thrust into this position, and apply themselves to so much in the face of adversity, they accomplish a lifestyle which is progressive and inclusive. Students are able to see inside lives and see the impact for people for themselves."

Jo Welch, *Senior Lecturer Department of Nursing (Children's Learning Disability and Mental Health) and Social Work School of Health and Social Work, University of Hertfordshire*

"Only last week I used part of Emma Murphy's story with a group of student nurses studying children's nursing at the University of South Wales. When I gave it to them to read I'd never heard such a quiet classroom! They found it really helpful in understanding the experience of parents being catapulted into an alien hospital world only to find that after a short time they soon became part of that world, offering support to other new parents. It also emphasised the importance of seeing families as part of the team supporting the child and how little things can be important (such as knowing how parents like their tea.) For me, having this resource to use in teaching was really helpful as the mums can convey the important messages much more clearly and forcibly than I can as it is their experience."

Ruth Northway, *Learning Disability Nurse/Professor, University of South Wales*

"I am a student learning disability nurse at the University of Hertfordshire with a passion for fairness and equality. People with learning disabilities are among the least empowered members of society when it comes to accessing the same quality of life and access to healthcare expected by the rest of the population. This inequality further impacts on the families and carers supporting them. Reading the Warrior Mum's stories has inspired me to ensure that in my future practice I really listen to the needs and wishes of people's families. Warrior mums in particular deserve better support from those who should be helping in order that they can use their strength in supporting their children rather than in fighting for what they need. Warrior mums to me are an inspiration; confirmation that behind every *label* there is a unique person and family with unique needs."

Maria Walker, *Student Nurse, University of Hertfordshire*

"I think the *Warrior Mum* blog series is amazing. It's about real life families and their struggles with their precious special needs kids who are certainly not helped by the very system that should make their lives easier. They are truly inspiring; full of love and admiration and will do whatever it takes to fight for what their child needs. The laughter the tears the pain, it's all there!

Reading about families who have the same issues as we have makes me feel less alone."

Sophie Sleep, *Minehead, Devon.*

"As the mother of a special needs child I found these inspirational true stories comforting, embracing.

I know the fear that accompanies being told your child has special needs—is disabled and vulnerable!

I related to the initial grief they experienced—their squashed expectations and shattered dreams—and I rejoiced (often with tears pouring down my face) with them as they spoke of different dreams, the thrill of watching their child make strides and reach milestones they feared (in the early days) they might never reach.

The *Warrior Mums* blog gives an insight into the struggles special needs parents face for those who don't know and offering of hope and encouragement for those who do!

Thank you *Warrior Mums* for sharing your stories."

Kimmie Edwards, *Essex*

"*Warrior Mums* could not be a more appropriate name. The mums who have written for this book are nothing short of inspiring. We all feel sorry for ourselves occasionally but what some of these women have gone through—and still go through on a daily basis—is truly humbling. Despite this, their courage and love for their family shines through. Truly they are warrior mums!"

Rebekah Julian, *Dereham, Norfolk*

"These stories have left me laughing, smiling, concerned and at times weeping. The range of emotions are the heartfelt responses to brave, noble and courageous ' Warrior Mums' who have all 'fought' for their family, often against injustice and always with pride and dignity. Women who have fought for others to see what they see in their children at last get to tell their story and we should all listen."

Nicky Genders, *Associate Head of School (nursing & midwifery)/learning disability nurse. De Montfort University Leicester*

"*Warrior Mum* blogs are inspirational, they make you smile, laugh and cry but most of all they make you think.

The blogs give you a rare insight into what life is like for families, fighting every day for their rights and to give their children a chance in life. They are a gift shared with incredible honesty from amazing people."

Hazel Powell, *Programme Director, NHS Education for Scotland*

"Warrior Mum's have provided me a great deal of personal inspiration throughout my education and subsequently as I moved into practice. Giving a voice to those who have fought and continue to fight for their children to have equal rights, and even the provision of basic care has resounded with my initial choice to come into Learning Disability Nursing. Every time I am now faced with a report or assessment on a person, I can't help but find my thinking of those Warrior Mum's, behind the scenes, tirelessly not giving in the fight to get the best for their child."

Ian Stevenson, *Clinical Practitioner (RNLD) Employed by NHS in Medium Secure Care, West Yorkshire.*

"I graduated from University of Central England (now known as Birmingham City University) in 1998, and started working in a residential/nursing home for adults with LD and behaviour which challenges.

My current role is as an Acute Liaison Nurse role in a busy acute hospital. I routinely see people when they are at their most vulnerable and poorly. This impacts on their carers, whether paid or unpaid, the carers are also at their most vulnerable when the person they care for is so poorly.

As I am now a parent and step-parent I feel I am able to empathise with other parents, but do I really know how a family carer for a person with LD is feeling? How they are treated by services?

I am so grateful for the insight and information I get from the Warrior Mum blogs, which for some time now have become essential reading for me. The points of view I get from parents of people with LD have made me a better nurse and a better practitioner, and I'm so grateful they're available to all."

Sally Wilson, *RNLD @salsa442 and founder member of @ WeLDNurses*

Warrior Mums

Other books by the author:

Marie's Voice (1992)

I Love Charlotte Brontë (2012)

With a Little Help From my Friends (2012)

Warrior Mums

Stories compiled and edited by
Michelle Daly

Michelle Daly • Liverpool

ISBN 978-0-9570487-6-8 (Paperback Original)
ISBN 978-0-9570487-7-5 (ebook)

All of the stories in this book have appeared on:
http://michelledaly.blogspot.com

Cover and book layout/design by MaryChris Bradley,
The Book Team, Edison NJ, USA.

Contact Michelle Daly:
Email: michelleannedaly@yahoo.co.uk
Twitter: @MichelleDalyLiv
Facebook: facebook.com/michelleannedaly
Blog: michelledaly.blogspot.com

To Marie, Patrick, and Anna, and to parents of special needs children and adults all over the world.

Contents

Acknowledgements iii

Introduction vii

Emma Murphy 1

Hayley Goleniowska 17

Donna Street 27

Clair Cobbold 39

Sandy Costall 53

Justine Bailey 69

Jo Worgan 83

Julia Donal 97

Wendy Hirst 115

Lesley Chan 129

Jane Raca 145

Acknowledgements

Thank you:

To all the women who contributed to this book.

To my Facebook and Twitter friends and supporters around the world.

To the learning disability nurse community for their feedback, encouragement, and enthusiasm.

To MaryChris Bradley of The Book Team, for her patience and professionalism—for going the extra mile in making this book something for us all to be proud of.

As Chief executive of the Royal Mencap Society, and also as a mum, I have the utmost respect for parents and carers, many of whom sacrifice a huge amount, but also gain a huge amount of joy and insight from caring for loved ones with a learning disability.

Family is at the heart of the Royal Mencap Society. We were founded in 1946 by Judy Fryd, mother of a child with a learning disability—65 years later, family continues to be at the heart of everything we do.

We are honoured that Mencap has been chosen as the beneficiary of this book. We are also humbled by these amazingly brave women who have shared their stories so powerfully. It is only by harnessing the love, positivity, and hope of all the people with a learning disability and their families, that we will be able to change things.

In your name, and in the name of all people with a learning disability and their families, Mencap will continue to fight to ensure that everyone has the freedom to live a life without fear and without limit,

Thank you,
Jan

Jan Tregelles, Chief executive, Royal Mencap Society

Introduction

My life has been easy in comparison to the lives of these incredible women. I never had the heartache or the feelings of guilt that a mother often feels after giving birth to a sick or disabled child. You see, I met my daughter when I was 16 and she was 5. The only disabled child in Nazareth House Children's Home where I was working as a housemother, she had been locked in the pram store room all day—every day—alone. Her cerebral palsy meant she could not walk and would drag her feet along the nuns polished floors leaving marks in her trail (and they couldn't have that!) Her severe learning disability meant her only stimulation was to scream and screech for hours on end, crashing her head onto the floor, leaving a permanent sore, blood constantly trickling down her forehead. When the home closed down later that year, Marie was sent to live in a big hospital where I was also offered a job as a cadet nurse. Though most of the staff were kind, I felt a hospital was no place to bring up a young child, so I left my job and contacted Marie's mother who made me Marie's legal guardian which—at the age of nineteen—gave me the power to bring her home to live with me.

Marie's early years left her with many fears and behaviour problems and one of her biggest fears was being left alone. It had taken many months and a lot of hard work to get her to finally sleep in her own room.

Like so many marriages, my first marriage broke down after only a few years and Marie and I went to live with my parents in Liverpool. We had single beds in my old bedroom and 13-year-old Marie was in seventh heaven being able to share with me. Some mornings my mother woke us with a tray of tea and toast and I'd squeeze Marie into bed with me while she ate her toast, passing her drink now and again then resting it back on the tray. I think we were quite spoilt!

The problem started when we began to live on our own again. Despite having a lovely two bedroom house and days full of fun and laughter, within half an hour of Marie going to bed in her own new bedroom she reverted to her old ways and the screeching began. She would scream and screech for hours and I mean hours. All the continuity with her bedtime routine had been wiped out. Sometimes there'd be a short lull and all would be quiet. I would creep up the stairs and open her door very quietly just to make sure she hadn't hurt herself. She would be sitting on the floor looking up at me, hair in disarray, mattress half off her bed, curtains pulled down off the windows, tutting at me as if someone else had done it. Today I wonder why I didn't allow her to familiarise herself with the change. She could have continued to share a room with me and slowly been introduced to her own room, but I guess none of us are perfect and I made a big mistake expecting her to adjust to being alone again when she hated it so much.

I can't remember how long it went on for, but I realised it was too long after my next door neighbour knocked on the wall calling for me to 'shut her up'. On a scale of 1 to 10, the psychological effect of Marie's screams on me was a 2. The neighbour banging on the wall was a 20. Our neighbour was actually very nice and apologised to me the next day, explaining she arrived home after a stressful day at work and snapped when she heard Marie screeching (again).

Over the weeks my nerves became jarred. My neighbour only banged on the wall that once, but once was enough to make me aware her peace was being shattered every night when the screeching began. I didn't know where to turn. Night after night I sat for hours listening to the screams, expecting the neighbour to knock at any time. I was twenty-five and trying to cope with a broken marriage and being alone again. I lost so much weight I was down to eight-and-a-half stone. Marie was trying to cope with the change too. I didn't know what to do anymore.

In desperation, I wrote to a consultant psychiatrist who specialised in learning disability and whom we had seen two or three times a year before we moved back with my parents. She was fantastic and so hands-on with the parents that I had her home phone number in case problems arose in between appointments. In my letter I asked the consultant if Marie and I could go and see her. However, we were 140 miles away and under a different health authority. She could have responded to my letter suggesting I see my GP for a referral to a local specialist, but she didn't. A few days later I received an appointment to go and see her almost immediately.

It's strange that I don't remember how we got to the station that morning after we left the house, or the train journey down to Peterborough. I felt dead inside. I just couldn't cope any more. I was going to ask the consultant if Marie could have a permanent bed in the residential facility she ran.

I have a clear memory of being in the consultant's office and Marie going into one of her screaming bouts. I couldn't do anything with her as she sat on the floor screaming, making it difficult to talk above her noise. I felt so useless, and so drained, and knew I brought the situation on myself. (Broken marriage—all my fault…)

On reflection, it was probably a good thing for the consultant to see Marie in one of her rages; seeing first-hand how difficult and distressing the situation was for both of us. I asked her about the possibility of Marie going to live in the unit. I was filled with shame. I loved Marie so much but I couldn't see any other way out.

The consultant was kind and concerned and I was sorry to have put her in such an impossible situation. She knew me well and said she didn't think I would like myself very much if I took those steps. She was right, of course. I began to realise that sometimes it takes other people to remind us of who and what we are.

We had a long chat, and after reviewing Marie's epilepsy and other medications, she suggested a lower dose more frequently instead of a high dose at night and she would write to inform our GP of this.

I *do* remember the train journey home that evening. We didn't get into Liverpool until after eleven. I left the house earlier that day full of despair. I returned feeling like I had been reborn. The doubt and uncertainty began to melt away and I decided we were going to be okay, and I was in it for the long haul. Within a few days of Marie's medication being altered, the screaming bouts stopped, and she gradually settled down at night.

But the experience made me painfully aware of the difficulties parents of disabled children face. A child that does not sleep wears you down with the sheer endlessness of it all, night after night. I was fortunate to have had someone to turn to.

That was in the late 70's. Today parents of special needs children would be lucky to meet a consultant psychiatrist let alone have their home phone number. Most of them don't even have access to a social worker anymore.

Then came the Internet! The good old Internet with its media sites and forums that gave us parents a voice that could be heard around the world. Many of us were full time carers and the support we gave each other was a lifeline—an opportunity not only to share the joy our sons and daughters brought into our lives, but also the chance to rant about the frequent injustices we met head on.

A lot of mums found an outlet in blogging about their daily lives, and as I read some of their stories the hair stood up on the back of my neck. I tend to read blogs rather than write them, but a burning desire to share their stories with a wider readership motivated me into convincing these women how amazing they were—they really had no idea —thus creating the Warrior Mums.

Initially, I imagined a couple of pages with a few photos, but the more I learned, the more remarkable I found each and every family, and the more I encouraged them to share the sadness and the joys of how their lives panned out.

The Warrior Mum journeys were featured in my blog every Sunday and became an immediate hit, read by people from all walks of life, and discussed on Twitter for days afterwards.

I am so honoured to have *met* these wonderful women and I thank them from the bottom of my heart for their generosity of spirit, for opening their normally closed doors—dredging up memories they probably preferred to forget—in order to help others.

I hope this book will be a journey of enlightenment.

For new parents: it may give you pointers, and lots of hope to know these mums once felt afraid and bewildered just like some of you do now, but they came through and grew to love, and accept their special needs child just like you will.

For professionals: some of you may have been involved in these journeys, and had a positive impact on the family's life. And for those just starting out, take these stories with you and remember, as Warrior Mum Donna Street says in her journey: You have a chance—an opportunity to do good, but you have to want to…

Emma Murphy

"**There** are so many, many, many times I've thought my son was dying. So many times I've begged, and cried, and pleaded with God. There have been the dramatic side-of-the-road giving-mouth-to-mouth-incidents, and the more *controlled* 20-doctors-and-nurses-around-his-hospital-bed-on-a-"crash-call"-with-a-resus-trolley-and-heart-paddles, to the "shit-he's-stopped-breathing" in-the-middle-of-dinner-at-your-mate's-house kind of events with Hugh. And there's the times that I've woken in the middle of the night, or early in the morning, too scared to check—just in case."

Emma's Journey

I was born in Birmingham in the late 70's to Irish Parents. I was their second child; their first—my sister—died in infancy just two years earlier. My three younger brothers and I had an idyllic childhood. Most of it seemed to be spent playing and having fun. Each year we'd spend our six weeks summer holiday in Ireland, we seemed to be outside all the time—I'm sure it never rained!

Mum and Dad worked hard, Dad as a machine driver and labourer, and Mum worked nights in a care home so she could be at home for us before and after school. It instilled in us a good work ethic, and I started work part time at 14 in a cafe. After leaving school and sixth form, I went on to university to study psychology and sociology, but I continued to work weekends and holidays.

2

M: Why did you decide to become a special education teacher?

Part of my course at university was about autism. I found it fascinating and wanted to learn more. My tutor was inspiring and he found voluntary work for some friends and I homeschooling a child with severe autism using a behavioural approach to learning, known as Lovaas.

It was hard work, but I loved it, and after leaving university I went on to use applied behavioural analysis (ABA) with a number of other children, but this time as a paid therapist. My then boyfriend, now husband, and I lived in Jersey for a year where I continued this work alongside working as a special needs assistant in a mainstream nursery, and part-time in a medical centre. Working with children made me consider a career in teaching, and when we returned to Birmingham, I decided to apply to do a Post Graduate Certificate in Education (PGCE). Unfortunately I failed to secure a place, but instead found work supporting parents of children with special needs through the Parent Partnership Services. Little did I know that all of these experiences would help me in later life!

I started teacher training a year later, and spent two years teaching in a mainstream primary. Initially, my intention was to get the relevant teaching experience, and then move on to train to become an educational psychologist. However, once in the classroom, I discovered I loved teaching but I was still very interested in autism and special needs, so when a post for a teacher in an autistic specific special school came up, I applied and was delighted when I got it. I worked there for six years and was intending to return part-time after having the boys, but Hugh's medical needs made returning to work impossible, and I had to resign in July 2011.

Sean and Hugh are my two wonderful boys. Sean was

born in 2009, a month before my dad, his namesake, died of cancer. It was obviously a very difficult time for the family, but knowing that my dad met his first grandchild before he died is a very special memory.

Sean is a delightful, confident little boy. He is incredibly funny with a great imagination and he makes me laugh every day. He loves running around, playing rough and tumble games, pretending to be a superhero, and playing with cars. Yet despite his boisterous, outgoing nature he is incredibly kind and gentle with his little brother and he shows insight, empathy and understanding beyond his years.

Hugh was born in 2010, just 14 months after Sean. Just looking at Hugh fills me with a warm glow. There is something so perfect about him, and just sitting and holding him can fill you with such peace. He seems to have a profound effect on people. Anyone who meets him falls in love with him. I am so incredibly proud of both my boys and love them dearly.

M: After all the experience you gained teaching special needs children, it must have come as a shock to find yourself on the other side of the fence with your own special needs child?

Hugh is severely developmentally delayed; he's nearly three and a half but still functions at below that of a six month old. He can't sit, stand, or crawl independently, is non-verbal and is registered blind. He is fed via a tube straight into his stomach, and has medically intractable epilepsy—his seizures are life threatening. It sounds ridiculous that after all my experience of working with children with special needs, that I was shocked to discover that such a degree of disability existed.

I've met and worked with children with severe autism, Down syndrome, and all manner of physical and learning difficulties, but I had never imagined what having a child as profoundly disabled as Hugh would be like.

On paper it sounds depressing. I think that if I had been presented with a list of Hugh's difficulties when I first began to suspect that something was *different* about Hugh, I'd have been terrified, heartbroken. But that list of all the things my son can't do, all the things that are wrong with him, tell you nothing about his wonderful, sunny personality, his smile that literally lights up his whole face, how he has the cutest giggle imaginable. He might be profoundly disabled, and have complex medical needs, but first and foremost he is a little boy; he is my little boy.

People often say that God only gives special children like Hugh to special people. But I believe I am the lucky one to have been given the chance to love such an amazing child.

M: I came across your blog, *The Unwelcome Visitor*, which

gives some alarming insight into Hugh's epilepsy…

Epilepsy made a sudden and unexpected late night call to our house last week. He hadn't been invited and I think it was a bit rude to turn up unannounced at 10:30 p.m. while I was enjoying a glass of wine and watching The White Queen.

It was sneaky, I think, to wait until the one night that I'd put Hugh to bed without the SATs monitor on but I caught him on the video monitor all the same. Hugh had had a lovely day at the farm—laughing at the noises the animals made, giggling when the sheep licked the food off his hands. I'm not sure why epilepsy wanted to spoil that. But He was angry and came in with a vengeance I'd not seen in a long time.

He tried to take my baby again. Three times Hugh turned blue, each time more and more navy than the time before. His little finger tips nearly black from the lack of oxygen; the SATs monitor screeching its high pitched warnings. I breathed life back into his lungs and begged him to come back to me. It's been 21 months since I've had to give Hugh midazolam, I could barely remember how much to give—maybe that was why epilepsy had waited so long; I'd started to become complacent, he thought he'd catch me off guard. But I did remember, just in time, and after four long minutes Hugh gasped for air and epilepsy left his body; weak, and pale, and breathing.

Hugh slept by my side all night; the still and lifeless sleep of the heavily sedated. I watched and waited; a lioness protecting her cub, ready to pounce should the predator return. And return he did, as the sun began to rise; first slowly, but growing ever stronger, lingering longer and longer each time. Trying again in the car on the way to hospital was a sneaky move, but I was prepared—oxygen at the ready.

At the hospital, first in resus, then in the High Dependency Unit, sedative after sedative was pumped through Hugh's veins, trying to flush the demon out. But time and time again he tried to take my son with him.

I prayed, and I cried, and I watched, and I waited. Not knowing what would be left of my son. Epilepsy had ravaged his brain before—taking his beautiful smile. It took Hugh two weeks to open his eyes, months to learn to hold his head up again. Powerless, I waited to see what devastation epilepsy had caused this time.

Once again though, my baby fought back.

Forty eight hours, twenty seizures, midazolam, clobazam, lorazepam and Phenobarbital, two crash calls, 'bag and masked' eight times, a collective total of 45 minutes of not breathing…and the little beauty came back to me."

M: Does that mean you're always on high alert, ready for a hospital admission?

In the first winter of Hugh's life, he became a regular visitor to the children's ward. I remember during one of those early admissions, talking to the nurse about his repeated visits and wondering if this was a pattern likely to continue. He'd had every illness going from chest infections and infected eczema to the more obscure cellulitis and swine flu. If you could catch it, Hugh would get it and he decided to further complicate matters by giving up breathing just before any illness would strike. Or while he was teething. Or indeed for no apparent reason at all. We later discovered this trick of going blue at inopportune moments was epilepsy. It certainly made winter *ahem* interesting, and acquainted us with the West Midland's Ambulance Service. It also meant we had our own bed reserved at Hotel Heartlands—a nice little ensuite, with views across the car park. The nurse confirmed my worst fears—that some children were season ticket holders, and became familiar faces on the ward.

Over the following year, I met a few of the regulars. You could instantly spot them—they were on first name terms with the nurses and helped themselves to bedding from the linen cupboard. They used medical sounding words, and spoke knowledgeably and confidently to the doctors, no shuffling shyly and deferring to the doctors clearly superior knowledge for them! I watched in fear and awe as they handled huge syringes, and pressed buttons on monitors with rapidly blinking lights, and important sounding alarms.

Hugh quickly secured his status as a regular with weekly, sometimes twice weekly admissions. He was presented with his loyalty card, granting open access to the ward. I was given a crash course in paediatric medicine, a learn while you work apprenticeship (though it was pretty poorly paid) supplemented by tutorials with Dr. Google. Now I'm the one asking for meds from the CD cupboard, with a collection of syringes on the bedside table, checking the oxygen at the bed stations, and adjusting the settings on the SATs monitors. Other patients look on in wonder as Hugh is greeted like an old friend with exclaims of, "He's grown so much," and nurses from neighbouring wards popping by to say hello, like he's a local celebrity. The parents glance slyly across as I attach purple tubes to beeping machines to hungry tummies. They turn away uncomfortable, and embarrassed as I set off angry alarms, and nurses and doctors come running with shouts of "crash call" and I'm pushed to the side while near-strangers try to save my son's life. They stroke the hands and faces of their own precious babies and silently thank God for *just* a broken leg, and *only* a chest infection.

And us regulars—war weary and battled scarred—smile a knowing smile at each other, a sad smile that says we've been there; we'll be back.

It has its upsides being a regular though: they know how you take your tea!

M: How difficult is it having two little boys, not that far apart in age, when one of them is often rushed to hospital in an ambulance. How do you explain that to Sean?

How do you explain to a four-year-old what a bag and mask is for? How do you explain to a four-year-old why his brother's not breathing? How do you explain to a four-year-old why you need to call an ambulance? What do you say when he asks how long it'll be before you come home?

Sean was probably around two and a half the last time we called an ambulance, three at the most. He'd seen it before, regularly, often, and it never occurred to him to worry. He didn't know any different. Ambulances and oxygen and hospitals had been part of his life for as long as he could remember.

But we had a reprieve, a break from all that.

And now he's four and a half. And he knows about emergencies and ambulances—they're taught it at nursery and school. Most children relate to it through things they've seen on TV—*Fireman Sam* and *Balamory*. Sean knows more than most.

He knows the paramedics come first in the smaller car. He knows that you have to wait a bit longer for the big ambulance—this one has the bed in it. He knows that a bag and mask is to breathe for you, and that sometimes Hugh's brain stops telling him to breathe. He knows that the blue lights and sirens mean it's an emergency and they can get to hospital faster this way. He knows his mummy has to go with his little brother in the ambulance to keep him company.

He knows we won't be home tonight.

And he takes all this on the chin as he always has done. But he watches the paramedics closely and asks what they're doing to his brother. He hangs around the bedroom door shifting from foot to foot as they take blood, check temperature, test heart rate, and monitor sats. He sees the wires, and tubes, and masks, and blood, and needles, and strangers surrounding his baby brother, and runs back in to watch *Tom and Jerry*.

Minutes later he's back. "I'll make a get well card for Hugh mummy" and he gives me a teddy to bring for Hugh.

M: Phew, it's such a lot for you all to cope with, Emma! Do you have any access to respite care?

Hugh's epilepsy causes him to stop breathing for prolonged periods of time, often as long as three minutes, but most recently he managed a full sixteen minutes only taking one or two breaths, which as you can imagine was terrifying. Leaving him in the care of others then, is something I find quite difficult—I'm always afraid they won't spot it in time. What if they go to the toilet or turn their back on him to have a conversation, and miss a seizure? He first started going to respite for four hours a week when he was about 8 months old, shortly after that he had his first seizure, although we didn't know what it was at the time—it took another 4 months before it was diagnosed as epilepsy. The staff were amazing though, and continued to have him for four hours a week. One member of staff was assigned to him and they'd sit and watch him for the whole session. He slept a lot and they would place a little soft toy on his tummy so they could see it move up and down, and be sure he was breathing. Each morning they would have a plan of who would commence mouth to mouth, and who would ring the ambulance. It was heartbreaking leaving him, but I needed that time with Sean. He was only two-years-old himself, and needed some time with his mum. I hated leaving Hugh, but knew Sean needed me too. I found places nearby I could take him—the park, a soft play area, I was never more than five or ten minutes away, and I checked my phone constantly.

As Hugh's seizures became more frequent, I found it impossible to drive with him in the car—I couldn't watch him, and drive safely, and so his four hours a week short-break sessions had to stop. Friends and family were trained in basic life support in an attempt to have him for a few hours, but he was spending so much time in hospital, and I was resuscitating him so regularly, that I daren't leave him with anyone anyway, and always felt it was far too much to expect anyone else to do that for him. Once I left the house to get petrol for the car, I was gone just over six minutes (I timed it) and when I got back Mum was giving him mouth-to-mouth. Since his seizures are classed as life–threatening, we were able to access support from the local hospice when he was about 18-months-old. He'd have day care sessions there, but initially I'd barely leave his side. Gradually, I managed to spend time away from him, first an hour within the same building, gradually building it up. He's had a couple of overnight stays there without me recently, though it still feels odd, and I worry about him a lot. We finally managed to get weekly respite organised for him just before his second birthday—a trained carer would come to the house and sit with him for a few hours just so I could have a shower or play with Sean in another room. Up until that point we had coped by ourselves. I say coped—I'd nearly reached breaking point! It's very hard to stay at that level of high alert constantly. I was mentally and physically exhausted.

Thankfully though—around the same time—Hugh's seizures started to become more controlled, and we didn't need to resuscitate him quite so often. Over time I managed to get him back into his short-break sessions (with his carer) and organised another four hours a week in a special needs playgroup—again with his one-to-one carer. I find it easier to leave him with a trained carer, as I know that he is their sole responsibility, and I've been lucky that the carers we have had have been absolutely lovely and he's bonded really well with them.

After a long period relatively seizure free, we thought we'd put the worst behind us, but he's had two hospital admissions in six weeks, needed resuscitating repeatedly, and a cocktail of anti-epileptics to stop them. He's proved that the risk is still there, and that he still needs one-to-one care. So although he is going to be starting a special school, where many of the children have complex medical needs, including epilepsy, and there are two school nurses on site, Hugh will still need his own one-to-one carer. The risks of missing one of his seizures are too great. We are in the process of organising that now. It's scary to think that he'll be away from me for such long periods of time, but I have to trust that other people will keep him safe. It's very hard though—his life is quite literally in their hands.

M: I've heard an awful lot about SWAN UK this year, how did you become involved with them?

Hugh still doesn't have a unifying diagnosis to explain all his complex medical needs, and developmental delays. Chromosome analysis has indicated a rearrangement of his chromosomes, but this in itself isn't enough to explain his difficulties. Genetics have looked for evidence of anything that might be missing, or duplicated, in his chromosomes but have yet to find anything. Initially, when we were told this, I was devastated. I wanted to know what was 'wrong' with him—something I could explain, something I could Google, something that would give me an indication of what the future held. Not knowing was frightening and isolating, and I genuinely thought we were the only people in the world without a diagnosis for their child. I searched the internet late into the night, desperately searching for answers until finally I found someone in a similar position without a diagnosis for their child.

At last I knew I wasn't alone. Some months later SWAN UK was re-established, and we both joined. It turned out there wasn't just one or two of us without a diagnosis, but in fact approximately 50% of children with learning difficulties don't have a diagnosis. It was such a relief to realise we weren't alone. The needs of the children all varied but the fact we had nowhere else to belong united us. I took an active part in the group, joined the advisory committee, and wrote posts for the newsletter and blog. All these things really helped me make sense of our experiences, and hopefully helped other people too. Perhaps more importantly though is the chance it gave me to meet other people who understood the fears and frustrations of our journey. I have made some amazing friends through SWAN UK.

M: I was delighted to see you and the boys on the BBC One National Lottery a few weeks ago. What was the appeal about?

The charity Genetic Alliance originally received five years funding from the National Lottery Big Lottery Fund which they used to re-establish the project SWAN UK. As a result of the amazing work they've done, SWAN UK was shortlisted as one of seven finalists in the health category of the

National Lottery Awards. Having the chance to represent SWAN UK in a short video that aired on the National Lottery show on a Saturday night was an honour. I was nervous that I wouldn't be able to do them justice, to show how much they had helped us, and people *like* us. It was all very exciting though. Although SWAN UK didn't win, it helped raise awareness of families living with undiagnosed conditions and highlighted the support available.

I'd like to finish my story with a poem I wrote for Hugh.

God Gave Me a Special Child

I am strong
Because my son has taught me to keep fighting
And never give up,
Even when it seems all hope is lost.

I am courageous
Because my son has taught me to trust my instincts,
To fight for what I believe in,
And not be too intimidated to make my voice heard.

I am humble
Because my son has taught me to ask for help when I can't do it alone,
To accept the things I cannot change
And to put the past behind me.

I am patient
Because my son has taught me that some things are worth waiting for.
Like that first giggle,
Or a smile.

I am thankful
Because my son has taught me to make the most of every opportunity,
To appreciate every day,
As if it were our last.

I am blessed
Because my son has taught me to see beauty in the world around me,
And that happiness, family and love
Are all that are truly important.

God didn't give me a child with special needs because of the gifts I had.
He gave me a child with special needs to teach me the skills I lacked.

Hayley Goleniowska

"I now understand the angst of those around me too, for medical professionals are also only human. My husband said he saw him shaking in the corridor. But looking back, a gentle word from a familiar friendly face might have taken the sting out of the thunderbolt. Would I have felt differently had we been told by our midwife after congratulations, while our baby was present?"

Hayley's Journey

I'm Hayley, first born of a hard-working couple in Sussex in 1969, followed four years later by my flame-haired brother Carl. Obsessed by horses and climbing trees, I was a more musical than academic child. I scraped into a grammar school by showing the examiner how to complete the Rubics Cube proving that kids' fads don't merely constitute a misspent youth.

I was the first person from our extended family to ever step foot inside a university. I went to Lancaster and studied an impractical mix of French Literature and Philosophy, but learnt the more important skills of research, independence and true friendship.

Various jobs followed, mainly teaching English to overseas students at colleges and universities. It was a job I loved, being a little bit of a stickler for good grammar despite my laid-back personality, and more importantly loving to meet new people from all over the world and learn about their lives and cultures.

I've also worked in a school as a teaching assistant. I was good at my job. But I now know I was not good enough.

My friends prefer to remember my hilarious stint as a voice-over artist for a premium-rate phone line which sold walk-though guides and cheats for computer games. Some still call me the Cheats Mistress but that is an identity I left far behind me long ago.

M: You're married to the lovely Bob; second time for both of you, tell us about your early years together, and the birth of your first child.

I married Bob, who works in the music biz, ten years ago and *technically* I am a stay at home mum of two beautiful girls. We planned a family straight away, a second marriage for both of us. After an initial early miscarriage, I was so proud to be pregnant again and after nine months of severe morning sickness Mia was born nine years ago; beautiful, dark and strong, with a wise, knowing face that looked as if she had *been here before*.

She instinctively and impulsively knew what she wanted out of life, and let everyone around her know. Believe you me she'll *get there*, wherever *there* is.

She is not only clever, musical, artistic, manipulative and bloomin' feisty, but the most caring, thoughtful and funny friend and family member anyone could wish for.

Often my thoughts turn to the crisp, sun-blessed December days just before our second child Natalia's arrival, when Mia and I planted daffodil bulbs together, enjoying every moment of mummy and first-born alone time that would never be repeated in quite the same way.

This was the time before our lives changed forever, the blissfully ignorant, arrogantly complacent time before we understood what life was really all about.

M: You've both been handed a question mark during your antenatal checks, how did you prepare?

We shrugged off a 1/297 nuchal fold risk (we now say chance or likelihood) of having a baby with Down's syndrome as not bad for my age, (35) and clung to the notion that a healthy, clean-living, vitamin-taking woman would, of course, be expecting another healthy baby.

She came early, as I instinctively felt she would. Two weeks early to be precise, typical for babies with Down's syndrome so I understand. The natural meticulously planned home birth was calm and straightforward. But a small, silent, blue baby was born on the bathroom floor, all in one easy movement.

M: What a shock for both of you, such a sudden birth. Tell us more about the arrival of your second child, and the journey that awaited you?

What followed is frozen in time.

The look of desperation on the midwife's face while my husband waited in shorts in a freezing lane for the ambulance. Jovial paramedics administering oxygen to our newborn and helping me to the ambulance. The midwife repeatedly telling me how beautiful she was as I held the oxygen to her face, a face I could not warm to, could not recognise as being my own baby's. Why did she keep saying that?

Hindsight brings sharply into focus that all these professionals instantly knew that Natty had Down's syndrome, but none of them could, or would, tell us.

On arrival at the hospital, my husband proudly carried

our baby from the ambulance to the second floor of the maternity wing. Our baby was quickly taken from us to NICU and we were ushered into a side room. I insisted that my husband stay at the baby's side while staff worked on her, which he did. Bob still cannot talk to me about exactly what he witnessed and felt during the next four hours, save that on several occasions he can recall the initials 'DS' being used.

But a strange thing happens when you are faced with what you think is your worst nightmare. You dare not welcome it in. You dare not let your brain begin to work out that DS of course means Down's syndrome. You absolutely will not let your head formulate a question to ask what is wrong, because you are terrified of the answer. If you don't ask, it won't happen, won't be real.

I was given no explanation of what was happening and began to feel that I was being avoided, that staff were afraid to come into my room, were avoiding something. As the hours ticked by, the panic began to rise within me.

Finally my husband returned with a smartly-dressed consultant. They both sat in chairs next to my bed while he delivered his pre-diagnosis.

"I've looked at your baby and I think she has Down's syndrome."

No one will ever fondly remember the delivery of unexpected news like this, but it felt too formal and too distant. Too much, too soon and overwhelmingly tragic. Talk of leaflets, a blasted poem about Holland, and meeting a nurse with a daughter with Down's all seemed to come at once with the adage that "some of them even go to school." Our midwife cried with us.

I wanted to scream at him, make him—and what he was saying—vanish, go home and start again, make a new baby. My life was over. We would never leave the house again, never go on holiday, Mia's life would be ruined. On and on my brain tumbled…

But I could not speak, only shake uncontrollably. He asked me if I had suspected. My head nodded by itself. Had I? So my core being had known all along. And all of this was done while "she" lay in a distant incubator in SCUBU on another ward.

I now understand the angst of those around me too, for medical professionals are also only human. My husband said he saw him shaking in the corridor. But looking back, a gentle word from a familiar friendly face might have taken the sting out of the thunderbolt. Would I have felt differently had we been told by our midwife after congratulations, while our baby was present.

She was our beautiful but vulnerable daughter first, with her fabulous, exciting life ahead of her. But telling us she had Down's syndrome amid tears and "sorrys" while she was out of sight and reach, meant that she became Downs' syndrome personified. My ignorance made her a frightening sum of all my ignorant stereotypes based on outdated glimpses into the lives of strangers with the condition, and the negative language and assumptions used by many in the medical profession compounded that.

M: You must have come across an array of professionals at this point, I'm sure some stood out more than others?

Key medical angels then came to the fore. The people whose faces and voices remain, whose influences are still felt in our hearts, yet whose names are long forgotten. Those who made us decide that our lives were far from over, and that we would make certain both girls reached their full potential.

The gently persuasive Sister who encouraged us to gradually look at, then touch, and finally hold Natty.

The kind nurse with a daughter with Down's syndrome willing to share a family photo album with us that soon made me realise that we would not only leave the house, but carry on going to all the places we went before.

The Junior Doctor who announced that he just knew we would be ambassadors for children like Natty one day. I remember looking at him quizzically through grieving eyes.

The Midwife who wisely told me that my baby needed my love whether she lived or died, and shook me out of my self-pity.

The GP, whose grandson has Down's syndrome. A no-nonsense man who welcomed her into his arms and coined her nickname Natty.

Knowing Health Visitor No. 2—Insensitive No. 1 was quickly bypassed—who had a child with a disability herself, who just *got it*.

The calm breastfeeding specialist who guided us through three tube-fed, milk-expressing months, until Natty finally succeeded for herself.

M: How is life now?

Natty won our hearts, grew stronger, survived heart surgery and flourished, as her proud father always predicted.

Her doting sister developed into a sensitive, caring, intuitive young lady, due to, not in spite of, her sibling's disability. I became an expert in every conceivable way of helping her reach her potential, spending hours reading and learning about the realities of Down's syndrome, yet sifting through mostly outdated data.

M: Tell us about your blog?

When Natty started school two years ago, I began writing my blog *Downside Up*. I wanted to offer support and encouragement to professionals and parents alike, for I know many of my initial fears were based in ignorance. I wanted to cut through the ancient narrative that is still being pedalled about trisomy 21.

I wanted to remove the fear and shock so that new parents wouldn't waste the precious early days coming to terms with Down's syndrome, rather than seeing their babies as simply that, first and foremost. I can't turn the clock back and make those early days as perfect as I wish they could have been, simply love that vulnerable baby who lay in the incubator for who she was, unaware of the stigma attached to her extra chromosome, but I can make up for it in other ways.

The blog quickly became popular, filling a needed gap I guess for there was nothing like it at the time. Natty began modelling, an ambassador for children with disabilities in her own right, around the same time, and that led to an ad inclusion campaign, and media interviews.

Since then I have followed the blog's path, it has been an organic process and it takes twists and turns I am never expecting. I'm always stunned that those who have nothing to do with disability also love to follow it, for they see that we all are more alike than unalike, that we can all relate to each other.

M: What do you think the future holds?

My days when the girls are at school have become structured, unpaid work. Dividing my time between writing guest posts and articles for charities, medical journals and magazines, doing interviews on TV and radio, giving talks to teachers and medical professionals or at blogging conferences, and writing to many parents, answering their questions in a friendly, familiar way. I've learnt to overcome my fear of public speaking and have been invited to give evidence in Parliament on the current disability abortion law. And this is more or less the underlying focus of the blog now. To change society's perceptions of Down's syndrome, to remove the fear, to change the assumption it holds that babies with an extra chromosome must be screened out at all costs, to show them that inclusion is a two-way street and that the value of our children, what they bring to society, cannot be measured in pound coins.

To Natty I say, "You have overcome obstacles that few can comprehend. You fought for your life in those first few weeks and learnt to breast-feed against all odds. You survived heart surgery. You have learnt to walk, and talk, and smile, and sing, and paint, and cook, and swim, and enjoy food, and ride horses, and make friends. Most of all you have changed opinions and melted stereotypes wherever you go.

You are our greatest teacher. Thank you for being, for slipping through those increasingly tiny holes in the sonographer's giant net."

To Natty

I love you so much and you are the best sister in the world and so precious to me.

You are so important to me and if you weren't in this world my life wouldn't be the same and that would be terrible.

So, I love you very much and you mean everything to me

Lots and lots of love from Mia x

Donna Street

"**Here's** your rainbow pack, a leaflet on the main autism charity in your area. Here's some information on family fund. Oh and here's your boxing gloves, your body armour, your chainmail vest, your lance and your cavalry horse for when you do battle. Hope you've got room in your boot? "Prepare for a fight" everyone said."

Donna's Journey

"I was born in 1978 in Birmingham with one sister. My parents were full-time workers, my mum a teacher and my dad a supervisor, and it was a very peaceful childhood with lots of holidays and the usual family parties! We had huge extended family so there were always lots of kids around to play with! I was very much into drama, and was a member of lots of amateur dramatics, taking on many a lead role. I continued this through my education and went to Aberystwyth University to study Drama."

Donna Street

M: What was your first job after leaving school?

Once I left university I went on to become an assistant entertainments manager at a holiday site both in England and abroad. I worked as an activity organiser at MIND for awhile, it was there I did my 110km charity trek through Guatemala! I travelled the Far East, and lived in India as a drama teacher, but eventually I returned to work in theatre in education, touring the country for about two years. When I met my husband I decided to settle down and became a drama teacher and children's entertainer in nurseries as Naughty Nancy the Pirate!

M: How did you meet your husband?

My husband and I met through a blind date and I have to admit it was love at first sight! I knew I'd met my soul mate, and we talked about raising a family all the time. We travelled the world for a bit but within three years we were married, with an Elvis impersonator performing at our wedding. I fell pregnant a few months later, but sadly we lost that baby very early on and the whole experience was very upsetting. I was told I wouldn't keep any pregnancies due to a medical problem but fell pregnant in the following year. Cody was born in 2008, and Jesse followed 10 months later in 2009!

 **Cody** is a deep thinking little boy with a cheeky sense of humour! He has mischief in his eyes and is a chip off the old daddy block! He was diagnosed with classic autism at 2½ and is non-verbal in a functional way, though his communication is getting better and he uses a lot of echolia in an ap-

29

propriate manner now. He's developed a taste for music, and is discovering strumming a guitar.

I like to say **Jesse** is brand new! She is curious about the world, and has a lust for life that is infectious! She always has the biggest smile on her face and her sensory seeking gets her into every nook and cranny she can reach and even some she can't! She has classic autism with significant learning difficulties, but don't tell her that as her rational and

logical thinking is astounding…there is nothing she can't work out how to reach! Nothing! Jesse is non-verbal but very, very, vocal! And has just discovered the joys of fairy wings!

My children are exceptionally happy, and very determined little people. They are truly a joy to be around even on the hardest of days!

M: Did you prepare yourself for a fight? Having two children with autism must have made your journey twice as hard? How easy, or difficult, was it to reach the diagnostic stage?

We were extremely lucky in the speed of our children's diagnosis though it was quite sad circumstances that lead to it happening as fast as it did. At the time of Cody's regressions I was starting my recovery from post natal pyschosis. I had been very ill, which meant there were a lot of health professionals lingering around our house at various times.

I remember one of them commenting on Cody not reacting when he bumped his head while she was there. That really started the process off, and I guess because of my illness things were hurried along. As they were assessing Cody it was very obvious Jesse was displaying traits too, so she literally followed Cody into the assessment process. Sadly, my illness meant that any fingers were pointed at me being the cause of the kids *problems* but I've learned to ignore such remarks now.

M: How do they get on at school?

The kids are in a local special school which has an excellent reputation. I was eager for them to receive specialised education as I knew they would not cope in a mainstream school. Before going to this specialised school they were in a wonderful private nursery that really adapted itself for our children who were the first SEN kids they'd had. But they went from there to special school last year, and now they are in the reception class. I cannot put into words the difference it has made to my children going to a school that truly understands them. The emphasis is getting them to learn through play, so although the staff are teaching Jesse and Cody basics like sitting down for a lesson, it's achieved in a fun way, and the kids are never forced into something they don't want to do. We tried hard to find a special school that didn't follow strict therapy guidelines for TEACCH or PECS, but rather let the children dictate their learning style. It's helped our kids become more confident and curious, which in turn, has brought on their communication and listening skills.

M: From the photos it's pretty clear you get down and dirty with the kids. Your background in Art, Drama and Mental Health, together with your sense of fun makes it all look so easy. Is it?

Oh no not at all! There are days we'll go to enormous effort only to be dismissed with a grunt—or worse—a full blown meltdown, and there are equally times when we really can't be bothered, but the kids want to climb all over us. My attitude of "stuff the mess" does help as it means I'm more open to trying things the kids seem to enjoy such as tipping, squirting, and throwing things on my floors.

It's a difficult choice between do I stop them, or do I grab this rare opportunity to interact? Most times I'll go with it because true *interactive play* doesn't come along that often and that used to deeply upset me. I guess that's why I over compensate sometimes by letting them get carried away, because I never thought it would happen.

So most of the things that have lead to the best times have happened by fluke…we just keep trying. For every one that works there's nine tries before that didn't!

M: Do you manage to have a night out together? I think the modern expression is *date night*.

Errr no! Not at all really. We have tried, but most times it has to be after bedtime as the kids won't go to sleep for anyone else, and by that time we're just too tired to get dolled up and go out! I'm extremely lucky to have Lee at home looking after the kids too (he gave up work to care for me when I was ill and then couldn't go back once the kids were diagnosed) so we make the most of our time in the day to put the house back together, and get ourselves ready for the kids home-time. So we get a lot of time together. I used to feel I was missing out not having date nights, but then I realise that we do get time to be by ourselves, just not how other couples do. But then, when has my family ever been normal?

M: I'll finish with this wonderful thought provoking piece

you wrote, Donna. I'm sure it echoes many a parent's sentiments—and thank you so much for sharing it with us...

Dear Professional,

I write to you as a mother. As a mother of children with a disability, special needs, learning difficulties, physical and medical issues, brain injury, challenging behaviour, sensory processing disorder, epilepsy, Down's syndrome, fragile X, cerebral palsy, autism. My children could be any of these, but the simple fact is, I write to you as a mother asking for help.

It may have taken me a great deal of bravery to come to you. To let you into my life, my child's life, my family life. I may be scared you will pass judgement on me. Maybe you will lay the blame at my feet. But I've climbed mountains, fought personal demons to do what is right for my family, and ask you to help me. Do not judge me, commend me. Do not scowl at me, smile at me. Make me feel like you will go the same distance for me, as I have travelled to get here.

My story did not begin when you entered my life, and it will not end there either. My story will continue long after you have walked away. But for that brief moment you are part of my story. Make it a positive experience. Write the chapter where you make change. Be that person we have been waiting for. You may be a supporting role or a starring part but they are equally important to me. The story is unwritten so add your own elements, and change the story for the better. Be the character I will remember long after you have left.

My children are precious to me. They are my world. I will never hurt, damage, break or alter my child, and you must not either. Embrace my child. Love my child for those few minutes, hours, days, or years, that you are with them. Treat them like there is no one else on earth. Show me you have their best interest at heart. Acknowledge them, play with them, show them you care. Take off your tie and play with them. Put down the clipboard and let them on your lap. Ask me how they are doing if they are not with me. Ask for photos and updates. Ask me what they can do instead of what they can't. Leave me on a high. The lows are already too great to bear alone. Be my shoulder to cry on, and I will sing your praises through my story.

Do not assume that you have the answers. Do not tell me you don't. Work with me, not against me. Think about what you say before you say it. Don't say it if you don't have to. Do not promise anything except your best effort, and in turn I will not criticise your efforts if they come from the heart. One size does not fit all.

Accept that I know my child. Listen. Trust what I say to be true. Do not disrespect those opinions without good reason. Nothing about me, without me.

I am emotional. I am tired, sad, angry, stressed, distressed, grieving, confused, optimistic, pessimistic, happy, content, dissatisfied. Sometimes all at once. Accept these emotions. Empathise.

Acknowledge my feelings in every meeting. Work with my emotions. Help me deal with them. Recognise that despite all of this I'm trying my best. Tell me you know this. Give me your time even though you have none. Go that extra mile. Support me appropriately. Signpost me accordingly. And I will thank you for it dearly.

Know that we are not in the same place you and I. You do not live this life, but have the honour of being invited in. Respect that. Do not try to second guess my needs. Ask me. Tell me you recognise the differences between us but will try to understand. Do not underestimate the strength and bond between parent and child. Know that watching my child meltdown, seizure, self harm, is not the same as watching *your* child meltdown, seizure, or self harm. You will never understand the lengths we will go to to stop that happening, so do not tell us to let it happen. Your expertise does not outweigh my experiences, but together they can be a power for good. Question with sensitivity. Leave your ego at the door. Learn from me and share your knowledge. Talk to me like a human but remain professional. This way you will gain my respect.

Leave me happy. My family helped. End it well. Say goodbye. Tie up all loose ends. Give my child closure and leave me satisfied. Know that you made a difference. Look back on your time with us fondly. Be proud to have helped.

Dear professional, you have a chance. An opportunity to do good. To create a union that will strengthen a family. To arm me with the tools to cope. To help me, help my child. To ease my emotions. To make my family a happier one.

But you have to want to.

I hope you want to.

A mother.

Clair Cobbold

"I remember the day my neurologist told me it was epilepsy. I think at the time the biggest thing was he told me I couldn't drive anymore. After another seizure I started medication. I was miles away from home, scared I'd have more seizures, and starting medication—lamotrigine—which initially had some horrible side effects (I would have panic attacks in my sleep.) It was a tough time, but I was determined to make it through university—and I did. By the second year my seizures seemed controlled, and my confidence returned, I got my driving licence back, and all seemed back to normal."

Clair's Journey

I was born in Guildford on 30th November, 1984. My childhood was pretty normal; I grew up in a small, close and supportive family, with my Mum and Dad, and a younger sister called Nikki. I loved junior school. I went to a very small school where there was a huge mix of different nationalities (it was a boarding school as well as a day school, I went as a day student) as well as abilities with children with learning difficulties and other disabilities.

I think it meant I accepted people no matter what their background, and that has stayed with me throughout my life.

My senior school experience was not so great. I didn't

really fit in, so just kept my head down, worked hard and ended up leaving with good grades which, looking back was the most important thing. I took a gap year working in a school, and became much more confident in myself which meant going to university wasn't quite as daunting.

M: Did you develop epilepsy in childhood?

It was a few weeks before going to university that I had my first major tonic-clonic (convulsive) seizure. All I remember is waking up very confused in a hawthorn bush and managing to stumble home. Because I had been out running on my own at the time, doctors thought I had fainted, and then bumped my head, and so I went off to university not really thinking much of it. A few weeks later I was out running with the athletics club when I had my second seizure, and ended up in hospital; that was when I really knew something wasn't right. I was referred to a specialist cardiologist (because it had happened whilst I was running they wanted to rule out a problem with my heart) who said she didn't think it was anything to do with my heart but ran the routine tests anyway before referring me on to a neurologist.

I remember the day my neurologist told me it was epilepsy. One of the hardest things to come to terms with was when he told me I couldn't drive anymore. After another seizure I started medication. I was miles away from home, scared I'd have more seizures. The medication—lamotrigine—initially had some horrible side effects (I would have panic attacks in my sleep.) It was a tough time, but I was determined to make it through university—and I did! By the second year my seizures seemed controlled, and my confidence returned, I got my driving licence back, and all seemed back to normal.

After leaving university, I went a couple of years without

any major seizures, then had one out of the blue. Since then it has pretty much followed that pattern; I seem to go a year or two without a major seizure, then just have one out of the blue. I don't get a warning, so it is always in the back of my mind that I could have one at any time. As time goes by, I become more confident, but I do worry about it especially now I'm a mum.

After a few more seizures I lost all confidence in my neurologist, especially after he told me the contraceptive pill didn't reduce lamotrigine levels when I knew it did because the drug company said so. I demanded to see an epilepsy nurse, and said I'd go anywhere for an appointment. In the end I was referred to the National Neurology and Neurosurgery Hospital in London. When my appointment came around I didn't think my epilepsy was serious enough for me to be there, and felt a bit like I was wasting their time, but it was a turning point in my care. For the first time, I felt like the doctor knew more than I did (I was always very good at researching my epilepsy online.) The nurse told me I was right about the contraceptive pill, and took me off it. She put my folic acid up to the correct dose a woman with epilepsy who may wish to start a family would require to help reduce the risk of birth defects, and found I had a vitamin D deficiency, common in people with epilepsy due to their medication.

But the most important thing she said is that I was probably having partial seizures as well. All my life I'd had these episodes, they lasted a fraction of a second, and are difficult to describe. They are sort of like a wave of emotion which washes over me, and then my vision changes briefly. People don't even notice I have them. They can never be sure they are seizures. They only happen once or twice every few months so will never be caught on an EEG, but

I had always thought they might be, and now a specialist agreed.

This changed everything. It meant I had never been completely seizure free. My medication is as high as I'm allowed, and I have been 2 years without a major tonic-clonic seizure, but I still have the odd partial seizure which I can live with. But it does mean it's always sort of there…

M: Did that mean an end to your outdoor activities?

I never let my epilepsy stop me doing the things I loved. I have grown up around horses as my family run a livery yard. I have had a few lovely horses in my life, but for the last 14 years—half my life—I have had Mac. I don't think I ever took him for granted, and always felt very lucky to have a horse I could rely upon so much.

He looked after me. He was so sensible, he wouldn't make

a fuss about things, and he was so much fun. We used to do gymkhana and he loved it. I always felt able to just go for a ride, think things through and get away from every thing for a while. My epilepsy didn't really bother me when I was riding Mac, and I knew he'd look after me should something happen.

But one Sunday night he had to be put down. It was

completely unexpected. He had a few health problems, but nothing major; he got a twisted gut and so my Mum had to make the incredibly hard decision to say goodbye.

It didn't seem real. I know some people will say, he's just a pet, but to me he was more than that—he was a friend. He'd always been there for me; horses never judge. He was there through the good times and the bad, when I was being bullied, and I remember when I was diagnosed with epilepsy I'd sobbed into his mane. He was a big part of all the best times of my life too. I remember revising for my exams on our Saturday rides with a friend. We'd write everything onto flash cards and take them with us. Whenever something great happened in my life I'd go for a ride all happy, and it would give me time to take it all in.

Mac changed my life and there will never be another horse like him.

M: Do you have much family support?

Without my family I don't know what I would have done. On a practical side, my mum would drive to and from Norwich where I was at university, but more than that she stood by me, supported me through the whole thing, and was always there for me. My dad would look things up and give me lots of useful information, and my sister was a true friend; we had always been really close.

Clair, Mum, Granddad

Another person who played a huge part in my life was my Granddad. I was very close to him and saw him all the time. Because I couldn't drive he would give me lifts everywhere, and it gave us a lot of time to chat and talk about everything. He died very suddenly two weeks before Riley was born. I found that very hard. I didn't really get a chance to come to terms with him passing so unexpectedly before Riley arrived and that made the first few months of being a mum very hard. I miss Granddad every day, but as time passes, the sadness turns to smiles at the precious memories I have of him.

M: How did you meet your husband?

It was during my lowest time that I met my husband-to-be: Rich. He was a friend of a friend. I met him when I went down to visit her at university. I remember we went for breakfast while my friend was at the doctors, and when I told him about my epilepsy I just broke down in tears. I expected him to run a mile, thinking I was some crazy girl. But he didn't. He supported me, even though he hardly knew me. After a while we started going out, but being on opposite sides of the country was a true test. We made it through university and moved in together. That was almost 10 years ago now. We got married 3 years ago; we had a small service in a country pub and a meal, then, went to Scotland for a week and came back and had a big party for our more extended family and friends. It worked really well. I didn't want to do it all on one day and get tired and risk having a seizure. Rich is my rock and is always there for me. We are a little team through the good times and the bad.

M: What did you study at university?

I did physiotherapy but I never really enjoyed it...maybe that was because I missed so much of my first year or maybe it just wasn't for me; I will never know. On leaving university the physio job situation was dire. So I took a job as a support worker at an epilepsy centre and then became an assistant unit manager. They never really worried about my epilepsy there.

During a period where I seemed to be seizure free I moved onto a rehab centre for children with brain injuries as a rehabilitation care assistant. I loved it, but then my epilepsy reared its ugly head and this time I wasn't allowed to work one to one with the children. I struggled on for a long time but it was frustrating and upset me how my epilepsy was effecting my work. Of course, I could understand they needed to protect the children but it broke my heart not to be able to work with them the way I was used to.

After returning from maternity leave I decided I needed to change jobs and do something that my epilepsy wouldn't impact on. I loved the place I worked, and all that was done for children with brain injuries and their families is second to none. A role came up as an online community co-ordinator, so for me to still be able to support families but online was absolutely perfect for my situation. I have been doing it for a few months now and I really love it; it has worked out perfectly for me.

M: How was your pregnancy?

In a nutshell my pregnancy was definitely a challenge. Six weeks in I had a major seizure, which wasn't a good start. The first worry I had was the possibility of birth defects from the epilepsy medication. Then, I had the added worry of how the seizure might have affected the baby. I was so terrified going for the first scan, and so relieved to be told all was running smoothly.

Epilepsy medication and birth defects is a difficult issue

for women to face; do you reduce your medication and reduce the risk to the child from the medication, but risk having a seizure and that affecting the baby? For me having a seizure at the beginning made that decision for me. I needed to make sure my medication levels remained high. I had blood tests throughout as drug levels tend to drop during pregnancy and so my dose was increased accordingly.

The rest of my pregnancy passed without any more seizures. I had lots and lots of different appointments both at the maternity hospital, and with my epilepsy specialist. I never had any of the choices other mum's might have had like home or water births, but I didn't mind, I just wanted my baby to arrive safe. I was lucky enough to have a clear birth plan. I took clobazam, another drug, during labour to reduce the chance of me having a seizure and had an IV put in as soon as I got to hospital so that emergency medication could be given if I started to seizure.

I had an epidural put in to reduce pain, and also to reduce the risk of a seizure, and to allow for a quick caesarean if I had a seizure. The labour was definitely not straight forward but had nothing to do with my epilepsy. My beautiful healthy little girl, Riley Elizabeth arrived—with a lot of help from some forceps—at 6 p.m. on Sunday 3rd June 2012—The Royal Jubilee. I was very lucky that one of my oldest friends was a student midwife at the hospital. She had followed my whole pregnancy, attending all my appointments, using me as a case study. It meant she knew exactly what had been decided by all the health professionals I had seen during my pregnancy, and she helped deliver Riley.

M: How are you enjoying motherhood?

I think that it's important to point out that the everlasting bond with your baby doesn't always happen straight away, and I think that makes you feel really bad about yourself. Having a baby changes everything, it takes time to adjust. I loved Riley from the beginning and wanted to keep her safe, but it took time to get that special bond between a mother and child.

Being a mum is a fantastic feeling. It has its tricky moments but as I watch Riley grow and learn new things, words can't express how proud it makes me feel. And the knowledge that I am her whole world, and the unconditional love she gives is truly amazing. I can't imagine life without Riley now; without her cheeky grin and goldfish kisses; she means the world to me.

Epilepsy doesn't stop me being a mum—my epilepsy nurse always made a big thing about that. It's all about weighing up the risks of having a seizure with being able to be a mum.

There are things I have done to reduce the risk to Riley. My parents bought me an epilepsy monitor so my Mum is contacted if I have a seizure. When Riley was little I would carry her up the stairs in her car seat, and I had a dead brake put on my buggy by a charity called re-map. I don't bath Riley on my own, I wait for Rich to get home, and I try to do as much as possible on the floor, for example, breast feeding, changing and feeding.

M: Is there anything in particular you feel holds you back?

Not being able to drive is hard. I think it can stop you getting out and about, and make you feel isolated. I made sure I never let that happen. I found local baby groups and enjoyed meeting other mums. I soon made friends who would come to my town to have a coffee to make it easier for me. By the time Riley was a few months old, we had the buses and trains all figured out, and now I can get pretty much everywhere. We are also lucky enough to have fantastic family and friends who look out for us, and will always give us lifts to places.

M: Sharing your story must inspire so many young mums and professionals. Do you get a lot of feedback?

I feel very fortunate for all the medical support I received and for the support Rich and my family have given me; I know for many women that is not the case. I started writing my blog and got involved in the Epilepsy Action HealthE Mum-to-be campaign to try to help other women feel confident, and embrace motherhood despite their epilepsy. I believe epilepsy shouldn't ever stop someone from being a mum.

There's so much to talk about, especially the myths surrounding epilepsy, and also the Epilepsy Action Pregnancy Campaign which seems to be reaching a lot of media.

Busting a Myth—you can't breast feed if you're taking epilepsy medication.

I've read comments from a few new mums that health professionals have advised them not to breast feed because of the meds.

FACT: Most mum's can breastfeed when taking epilepsy meds.

There are a couple of meds that are an exception, and it's important to talk to your specialist or epilepsy nurse before the birth so you have your own understanding of the situation and stick to your decisions, whatever anyone else may say later on. It's so unfair to be told you can't breast feed after the birth only to be told a few days later you can, by which time it can be very hard or impossible to start.

If you think about it, the baby has been taking a small dose throughout your pregnancy; the small amount in your milk is negligible when they are growing so fast.

I breast fed until Riley was 16 months. I was a bit worried about night feeds and seizures because I was tired, however, we always agreed that if I was too tired Rich would help at night either with expressed milk or formula but it turned out I was ok.

Breastfeeding's not for everyone; it can be hard. I found the first few months a challenge, not due to my epilepsy, just normal mum things, but after 3 months it became easy. The main thing is you have the same choice as everyone else, having epilepsy doesn't change that. But never think just because you don't breastfeed you don't develop such a strong bond. People who say that are very unfair; it's not for everyone but don't let your epilepsy affect that decision.

I hope that the campaign, and being able to tell as many people as possible my experiences of pregnancy, and being a mum, will help women feel more confident and less alone. Hopefully it will also help health professionals have a better understanding of epilepsy and pregnancy, and some of the issues and worries women with epilepsy face during pregnancy and as a new mum.

M: Finally, I hear you were on the front cover of the Guardian Epilepsy Supplement in May—that must have been exciting.

The Guardian newspaper published a supplement dedicated to epilepsy to support National Epilepsy Week—turns out we're on the front cover! I didn't realise it was going to be the main part of the cover, thought it would just be a little bit in the corner! It's great to see that pregnancy and epilepsy is being covered so much. Hopefully it'll make a difference to lots of other women out there. I feel quite proud to be so involved in the campaign.

I think every parent worries about their baby's development. I know that all babies develop in different areas at different rates but at the end of the day almost all of them reach the same point eventually. I guess I worry about it from an epilepsy meds point of view. In the back of my mind there is a little niggle—what if my AEDs have had some more long term effect on Riley. But the truth of the matter is Riley is developing like a normal child would, she's not been the first to walk, or the first to talk, but she is reaching all these important milestones, and I think the more she achieves, the less worried I become. She is truly amazing and I am so, so proud of everything she does.

I love being a mum. Watching my little girl develop and learn new things every day is amazing. I never thought I could love someone like I love Riley. I want to keep her safe, want to show her the world, and the fact that I am her whole world is a pretty scary, but I feel very lucky that she trusts me so much. We have so much fun together, we go to baby groups, picnics, play in the park, and I have made so many wonderful friends in the mum's I have met through her; she is my whole world. Okay, I have epilepsy, but to Riley I am just her mum. It does mean that some things have been more of a challenge. I have had some extra worries through having a child, but I would hate it if epilepsy stopped any woman from experiencing the most amazing feeling in the world…being a mum.

Sandy Costall

"It took me a long time to come to terms with Matthew not being the *perfect* baby that I had anticipated. I say perfect because I really was that shallow and self absorbed in my 20s. It was by meeting other parents and meeting their children and hearing their stories that it hit me—Matthew is perfect."

Sandy's Journey

I was born in Liverpool and have always lived on The Wirral—just across the River Mersey. I had a lovely stable childhood, and Mum and Dad worked hard to support me and my younger brother. We weren't rich, but never went hungry, and always lived in the same house. Mum and Dad brought me and my brother up to respect ourselves and other people, as well as sound morals and values.

My brother and I often quarrelled when growing up—we are both very different personalities. As we've got older and had our own children, I think we have become closer than we once were. I enjoyed going to school, and loved reading books, and learning from an early age—something that I still enjoy now!

M: What type of work did you go into when you left school?

When younger I was always interested in the sciences, so after leaving school I had continual employment in the local chemical industries. In 1998 whilst in my 20s, I gained my degree in Chemistry via day release, and moved to a local pharmaceutical company. I really enjoyed working in industry and was very career orientated. I've always been interested in continual learning and development. Whilst employed in pharmaceutics I studied counselling skills, and did a GCSE in Psychology. On reflection, I left school not really knowing myself what I wanted to do, but knowing that I enjoyed being round other people, and wanted to work hard, and achieve lots with my life. I've always had a strong sense of right and wrong, and have often taken on advocating for others.

M: Tell us about your husband and how you met him.

I met my wonderful husband, Andy, when we were both eighteen. He was a friend of a friend, and we hit it off straight away, married eight years later, and have been together ever since.

My husband has worked for the same chemical company since he was 17. He started out making the tea and coffee, and painting floors, and is now a senior manager who knows the business inside and out. He also achieved his degree via day release. Andy is the rock that keeps me grounded and focused when I start to get carried away with ideas or suggestions. He still makes me laugh after all this time together. Having a child with a learning disability has brought us closer together and Andy is a brilliant dad.

M: Tell me about Matty and Sam.

We have two boys: **Matty** is 13 and has Down's syndrome. He is every inch the teenager—mood swings, interested in girls, his appearance, socializing and playing video games!

Sam is 10 and will be starting secondary school in 2014. Their birthdays are 3 years and 3 days apart in July!

M: Did you carry Matty to full term?

I had a horrendous pregnancy with Matty—I was 28 and at first was in shock and denial. This was overshadowed by an extremely bad morning sickness which lasted all day every day throughout the pregnancy. At 33 weeks I was huge, and was feeling more and more unwell, I developed symptoms of pre-eclampsia so was admitted to hospital. They carried out a whole range of blood tests and monitoring, but couldn't find what was wrong with me. When they scanned the baby, they discovered that he had real problems, and it was the poor little mite who was making me ill. His body was producing excess fluid, and it had collected in his lung cavity.

M: That must have been an awful scary time for you.

I will never forget the doctor's face, and look of horror as he saw Matty's lungs floating in the fluid like soggy tissues. There was no way his lungs could survive outside my body.

But in his favour, at 33 weeks Matty was fully developed and a good size—he weighed 7lbs 10oz at birth—his heart showed none of the medical problems typically found in babies with Down's syndrome, and he had no bowel or stomach problems. They carried out in utero surgery to drain out the excess amniotic fluid to try and stop me going into labour, and to take the pressure off my kidneys. But the next day when they scanned and measured me, the fluid was back and Matty was fighting to stay alive under the pressure of the fluid. I was lucky that I had a fantastic consultant who had recently returned from London where he had experienced a new technique of operating on babies in utero to place shunts into a baby. So to save my baby's life, and give him the best chance of survival, we went through surgery. The consultant put in tiny shunts to drain the excess fluid out of Matty's lung cavity.

M: Was the operation successful?

The surgery was successful on the day, but when scanned the following day the fluid had returned, and a decision had to be made on what to do for the best. At that point we still did not know Matty had Down's syndrome. Finally the results of all the blood tests came through—we were taken to a family room in a quiet area of the maternity unit, and two consultants and a senior midwife broke the news, not only that our baby had Down's syndrome, but that he was producing the excess fluid as a direct result. They gave less than 20% chance of survival at birth, but said that they would do everything in their power to deliver him alive, and then operate to put drains into his lungs straightway, and put him on a ventilator in an incubator, and transfer him to the special care baby unit intensive care room.

M: It sounds like the medical team handled you with lots of support and sensitivity, but I don't suppose it helped to ease the shock?

It's strange how your brain shuts down when you receive shocking news—I will always remember staring at the clock just behind the doctor's head as she spoke. It was a run-of-the-mill NHS silver clock that ticked by quietly. The time was 1:33 p.m. and it was a hot July afternoon—I became aware of the tree outside, its reflection dancing across the wall and the clock face. A bus stopped outside the maternity unit across the road, and again I saw its distorted, broken reflection in the clock and wished I was on that bus—going far away from the nightmare. My life felt as broken and distorted as that reflection, and I stared back at the doctor not knowing what to say to her. The only sound was the soft ticking reminding me that my life had changed forever.

Everything in life we had taken for granted was suddenly snatched away. A date was set for surgery two days later to allow time to prepare the medical team of doctors, nurses, and midwives. I was discharged home for the weekend to help me come to terms with the news that had rocked our world—and the uncertainty of the path ahead. Andy was with me throughout and our families were as shell shocked as we were, but gave us amazing support and strength. So the obstetrician drained out as much of Matty's lung cavity fluid as he could, and the surgeon then delivered my baby via C section as Matty had shunts coming out of his sides he would not have survived a normal delivery. As soon as he came into the world the paediatric team took over, operating on him behind a screen in the same operating theatre. They got him breathing, inserted the drains to start pumping the fluid out of his little body and put him on a ventilator and soon after brought the incubator round to show me and Andy our new son. He was so puffed up with fluid that any features were difficult to see, but he had a beautiful mop of dark hair and the sweetest little mouth.

M: You must have had such mixed emotions when you looked at your little boy.

I had real difficulty in being a new mum. I felt like a failure—to my husband, to my family, and my baby. I felt numb inside—no one to talk to, even when surrounded by well-meaning family and friends, I felt so alone and traumatised. There was my baby lying in an incubator downstairs, and nothing I could do would actually help him live; he was only alive thanks to the machines breathing for him and the one-to-one nursing care he received.

M: Were you able to go and see him?

Other than first seeing him in the operating theatre, I couldn't bear to go and see him. Close family and Andy visited Matty in the special care baby unit that first day but I couldn't. I was scared. I didn't understand what was going on. Matty's doctors and nurses came to see me and Andy, and explained how our son was doing. I couldn't take it all in. The next day a wonderful ward midwife and a nurse from the baby unit entered my room and informed me I needed to see my son. I stared at the wall, and couldn't move. They did an intervention that I will always be grateful for—they washed, dressed, and did my hair for me. They made me feel like myself again. They then put me in a wheelchair, but all the while I sobbed, and sobbed. I told them I was scared in case my baby died. I didn't understand—why me? Was I being punished? The guilt I felt for Andy, and our families is indescribable, and the sadness of not having a prefect birth and baby.

I felt no immediate overflowing love, and I didn't know why. They were brilliant in just telling me I wasn't a failure; that it was okay to feel this way, and that no one can predict when things will go wrong. But it's happened, they told me, and you have a son who needs you right now. They were the tough love and care I desperately needed to start making sense of the situation.

M: How was Matty coping?

Matty showed us all, and he hung on and fought for life—amazing all the medical staff. Over the weeks his body gradually stopped producing the fluid, and his lungs began to work. My baby began to breathe for himself. The shunts that were put in prior to birth had slipped inside his body shortly before birth and settled into the lung cavity tissue. It would be too risky to remove them, and today they are part of his body and pose no threat or risk to him. Only one thing—Matty cannot have an MRI scan due to the metal contained inside them which would vibrate and resonate causing damage to his lungs.

I was given amazing support by the midwives and nurses in special care baby unit to help bond with Matty. As a mother who had gone through a trauma, they helped immensely. They really saved my sanity.

They also involved Andy, and both sets of grandparents, which meant so much when the normal ways of caring for a new baby are not always possible. We would be there to provide comforting words, and touch, after painful procedures had been done. We'd watch our little baby's heart rate decrease on the monitor. Our little boy knew he was loved, and we were there beside him.

At 12 weeks Matty was allowed home with oxygen support and made amazing progress. It's quite frightening, taking full responsibility of your baby after so much medical intervention. By the time he was nine months old, he was off the oxygen cannula's completely and his sat's were 99%—given when he was born his sat's averaged around 68-78%; he was amazing!

Although there were no heart problems, Matty still suffered with continual trapped wind and projectile vomiting. The medical assessment showed nothing to indicate any underlying health problem and the doctors advised it would most likely be due to his low muscle tone which affected every muscle, ligament, and tendon. Everything was affected. As Matty made good progress we were becoming less worried by his medical diagnosis and concentrated more on just being good parents.

Having a diagnosis at birth almost made things 'easier'—maybe that's not the right word, but having a diagnosis at birth means that the required professionals are there straight away.

Matty had physiotherapy, occupational therapy, speech therapy, portage, and lots of exposure to social situations from an early age. We were also signposted to our local Toy and Resource Library where mum's of other babies and children with Down's syndrome met each week. It was the lifeline I so desperately needed—other mum's who understood the endless round of challenges Matty faced because their children had similar ailments. The low muscle tone, poor cognitive abilities, difficulties in eating/drinking, and bowel managing. Matty struggled with his stomach and bowels—frequently vomiting after feeds, slow drinking and feeding coupled with bowels that moved very fast giving terrible trapped wind, plus the continual rounds of hospital visits and health assessments.

I made a few close friends, and made my own small support group of other mothers of special needs children. My son rarely slept—it was exhausting. The lack of sleep and a baby that needed continual feeding, then changing, physiotherapy, and medications, took its toll on us. I developed severe postnatal depression, and Andy developed severe depression. We were helped by family and professionals, and gradually recovered.

It took me a long time to come to terms with my son not being the *perfect* baby that I had anticipated. I say perfect because I really was that shallow and self absorbed in my twenties. It was by meeting other parents and their children, and hearing their stories that it hit me—Matthew *is* perfect. He is his own person, and such a strong personality.

I am so proud of him because so much is a struggle. The world can be a strange place for him, so I've become proficient in sensory processing disorders—something I'm always keen to learn more about, and utilise with my patients.

M: How do Sam and Matty get along?

My boys are feisty and very rough and tumble—typical boys really! They both have a massive sense of fun, and love life! Life with my children is never dull or quiet, and I learn so much from them, and am very proud of them both. Being a child with a sibling who has a learning disability brings its own challenges and frustrations for Sam. But they get on really well together, yes, they argue like most siblings, but once the argument is over, they are back to being best friends.

From an early age Sam had to go to Matty's hospital appointments, activities, and parties. Matty never seemed different to Sam. When he was old enough to ask questions about Matty's behaviours, different speech, and looks, we answered them all as best we could, and Sam has grown up with a mature and caring personality, and he loves to help people. Matty is also very caring and loves helping people, and both boys enjoy being in their local scout group. Their dad always missed giving back to his local community after scouts had given him so much when he was younger, so he joined the scout group where we live to help support Matty. It's been the best thing for my boys and their dad. I love watching them learn new skills, and build strong friendships, as well as being part of the local community, scouts also gives them regional, national, and international identity.

M: How did you manage to return to work?

I returned to work when Matty was six months old and he went to a local day nursery for half days. My retired parents cared for him in the afternoon's—often doing his Physio, speech therapy, portage exercises, and taking him out to experience the big world. It did him the world of good and was the foundation for the best start ever. He continued to make great progress, and eventually attended our local mainstream primary school with one-to-one support. However, it was a struggle, and hard work not only for Matty, but the school, his dad, and me. He did really well, but by the end of year 5 we knew that the gap between Matty and his peers was too wide to bridge, and we chose a local specialist sports secondary school for him. He was accepted by a school that had never had a child

with Down's syndrome before, and he still remains the only pupil with DS. We chose the school based upon Matty being an independent young man, holding his own in a classroom environment, and being able to form his own friendships within peer groups. It's been a challenge, and initially he started the school with some very challenging behaviour, but we worked with the teachers to promote positive interventions. Today, he is really settled at school, and is in the process of choosing his options. He's hoping to take some GCSE's and entry level qualifications!

Oh, and at his annual education statement review in April 2013—he was 12 at the time—his teacher presented us with a document Matty had written.

When asked to write his hopes and dreams for his life he wrote the following:

> "To have a job—in a pub so I can drink beer with my dad. I want to learn to drive so I can drive my own car. To have a girlfriend, to get married, and to have my own house and my own TV."

M: How is Matty's health?

Matty still faces health problems, but he takes them all in his stride and his dad and I juggle working full-time with being parents, and health appointments.

I've lost count the number of doctors or health professionals I've debated with when Matty has needed treatment, and I've had to ask them to talk to him, and not to me. He may still be young, but he knows his own body, and understands when he is in pain or discomfort. Although not able to speak very well, we use board marker symbols, and familiar photos to help his communication.

M: I bet when you looked into Matty's face when he was born you never imagined you'd become a learning disability nurse.

As time went by, and the more interesting and inspirational people I met through having Matty, the more I realized I no longer loved my job and wanted to do something else. It was my neighbour and close friend—a former nurse and midwife who had retrained as a university lecturer—who suggested I return to university; she thought I would be a great learning disability nurse. Before ever having Matty there was no way I'd have ever considered being a nurse.

But she really convinced me to put my life experiences, and people skills to good use by retraining. I took that leap of faith, and applied for voluntary redundancy, and in Jan 2009, I walked into the University of Chester School of Nursing.

M: I see you've also been involved with POSITIVE CHOICES, which for those who are unaware, is the only conference designed to enable learning disability student nurses from all over the country to celebrate the contribution they make to the lives of people with a learning/intellectual disability. I went to the event at Cumbria University earlier this year, unfortunately—due to a family bereavement—I could only stay a short time. I met Helen Laverty, and Michelle Parker, to name a few, and was bowled over by the student nurses I met from all over the country.
Am I right in thinking you also gave a presentation at one of the annual events?

Whilst in my second year at university I made contact with Helen Laverty and POSITIVE CHOICES, via Facebook. Helen is a Health Lecturer in learning disabilities at Nottingham University and she really inspired me to share my story of how I became a student learning disability nurse. I gave a 20 minute presentation at Leeds University and told my story to hundreds of gathered students. From that moment I knew I had met kindred spirits in those nurses, lecturers, and students.

Three months after my Leeds presentation, I won a place at York University as a finalist for the Fiona Law Student Nurse Award. My good friend, Graham Burrell, won the award, and under Helen's guidance we started a piece of research with the support of our two Universities (Chester and Cumbria) on the importance of student learning disability nurses networking during, and after their training as professionals. To date Graham and I have jointly presented at Hertfordshire, Bangor, and Edinburgh University. Our research data collected in 2011 needs calculating, and writing up. Unfortunately, working life has conspired against us ever seeing each other, and having time off work, to complete our research. One day we will complete our work—an initial article published in 2012, but we want to publish the whole report.

We have met some amazing people during the conferences, and hopefully inspired other students to start networking during their training.

POSITIVE CHOICES recharges my nurse batteries, and keeps me in touch with what's happening with students, and best practice. Helen Laverty, Jo Lay, Jo Welch, and the other people who organize the conference are truly inspirational. I really am inspired, and grateful to them for their support, belief, and encouragement to myself, and every other student that they meet.

M: I think you're fantastic to have achieved all you set out to do. How does it feel being a full-fledged learning disability nurse, and tell us about your graduation day.

I had very mixed emotions on my graduation day—on one hand total joy and pride with what it stood for, and for all that I'd achieved just to get there. To see the faces of my family and friends made it so special, especially getting congratulations from Matty, Sam and Andy. It made all the long hours, and sacrifices, worthwhile. It was also tinged with the sadness that my dad wasn't there to celebrate—just before he died, he'd made me promise to finish my nurse training, and that had kept me focused during the months after he passed away. It was also sad because a graduation marks the end of an amazing adventure of being a student, and the start of back to working for a living. It means that the road you've been walking has another path to follow, and starting out on the road as a fully qualified RNLD was scary. I knew everything would be okay because I'd worked hard as a student, and already had a job by the time I graduated three months after qualifying. I really enjoyed my graduation day—seeing my fellow new nurse friends who I'd spent the past three years with. Chester Cathedral is a wonderful place to graduate from. As I went up on stage, I caught a glimpse of my family's faces in the crowd, and Matty standing there cheering me on! My fellow students, and friends, waved and cheered, and as I came off stage, I saw all my lecturers who had been there for my journey. They had been immense sources of support and guidance throughout—especially when I doubted myself and my abilities as a student nurse. They cheered, and I punched the air. I'd done it! I'd made it!

I try to give back to everyone who helped me, as much as possible, as well as supporting students myself now. I'm proud to be a learning disability nurse, and am still aware of how much I don't know, and have yet to learn, but each day is a learning experience!

Justine Bailey

"**I** was a mother bear possessed at the beginning! I was not going to let this beat us. I was going to fight, scream, and get results whatever it took. What I didn't do too well was the bereavement, grieving for the child I could have had, and all the emotions that are tied up in that one word. That train crash happened sometime later."

Justine's Journey

My childhood was very complex! In fact, it's taken years of counselling to be able to talk about it.

I was born in Margate Queen Elizabeth, The Queen Mother Hospital, in Kent, quite some time ago. Somewhere between 3 and 4 years old, my parents separated. I can safely say it was a difficult marriage towards the end.

I have glimmers of happier times but they are few and far between. I remember the night we left my father really clearly; creeping out in the middle of a cold night, me, mum, and baby sister. We walked, and walked, and the only bit I remember with any clarity is walking along the sea front. I believe we were heading for the train station. A taxi driver pulled over to make sure we were okay. I'm sure it must have been an unusual sight in the dead of night, a woman, a toddler, a babe in arms, and a suitcase.

I was too young to know the ins and outs of it all. I have some memories of relatives' houses we stayed at, and lots of moving about. The significant chapter, though, when everything changed for me, was a trip to see my father, and grandparents (who I adored). It was only supposed to be for a week, but they kept me with them, and I never returned to live with my mother, and my sister, not as a young child anyhow.

My father refused to let me go back to my mother, and no amount of intervention changed the situation. So there I stayed. A very messy divorce and custody case ensued— one in which the Judge decided that in the interests of the older child (me), I should remain with my father! I would love to meet that man today. I would have a few choice words to say to him, and the social worker!

I could write a book, and there still would not be enough pages to capture the unhappiness, despair, resilience, and hope I've felt. I have carried that 4 year-old child with me my whole life; it's not easy letting her go.

Yet it wasn't all doom and gloom. There were enjoyable moments, but sometimes it's a struggle to find them. I loved to sing and dance. Some of my great memories were putting on shows with my friends, entering talent competitions, and just generally larking around, showbiz style! Those were happy days.

Things changed again for me when I was 15 and my younger sister miraculously re-appeared in my life. She'd rooted in our Mother's attic, and discovered that she had an older sister, and another dad. Her relentless determination to meet us gave me an opportunity of escape back to my mother's. Unfortunately, my younger sister is no longer with us, but I have so much to thank her for.

With that all said, everything that defines me now as an adult stemmed from that childhood; all the decisions and choices I make now, come from that childhood, and the way I want to be as a human being, comes from that childhood. I wouldn't change the past, even if I could.

M: What was your first job after leaving school?

When I moved to the North I was in the middle of my CSE's, but I did manage to do most of them—apart from English—before I left. I had dreams of becoming a nurse. My mum was really good at getting organised, and within months I was enrolled in a Pre-nursing course at the local college. I completed the first year and got my O' levels, including English, which I was quite chuffed about. Towards the end, however, I became somewhat disillusioned by the length of time it would take to become a fully fledged nurse so I opted out. I had already done two years typing at school so I signed up to a local YTS scheme. I quite liked the idea of earning money, and started working for a freight forwarding company.

M: Tell us about how you met your husband.

I met my husband Jonathan through his friend, who just happened to be a colleague at the freight company where I worked.

I was trying desperately to re-invent myself. Why then did I agree to a blind date? Fate only knows!

Jonathan was different to all the other guys I had met and that's what drew me to him. He was kind, slightly aloof, quirky, solid, and dependable. I'd put him through the ringer a few times just to see if he would walk, but no, he stayed put!

M: You have two teenagers?

Yes. **Elizabeth** is simply gorgeous! She is at University studying Fashion Promotion and Styling, and has this ornate way of doing things. I love her creativity and expression.

She is fantastic at photography, and I claim that side of her personality comes from me! When she was younger, we used to go out shopping and do brunch in Selfridg-

es. I suppose I wanted her to experience everything I hadn't as a child, so to some degree she was indulged. When her brother came along, we continued to do those things, it was really important for her that we had time together.

Regrettably, this did change though when it became clear that Robert was struggling. He seemed to take so much of my time, and she was becoming an independent teen, so those special outings together became few and far between.

Elizabeth treats her brother in the same way any neuro-typical sibling relationship would be. She doesn't see his autism as him being different, just a quirk that makes him **Robert**.

I so wanted a little boy. When I found out I was having one, I just went blue crazy. Oh, I had so many dreams for him. Along he came, and such a delightful baby, and so good at sleeping—he didn't really cry very much. I felt blessed.

M: When did you start to be concerned about Robert's development?

It all started with little things first, baby asthma, baby eczema, and an allergy to cow's milk. Then he started to struggle developmentally with his speech. I was still working while all this was happening, and the guilt was unbearable. A lovely SLT decided that at 26 months Robert wasn't really that far behind his peers in speech, and that it was probably because he was a boy and lazy! Never mind the fact he couldn't ask for the basics like juice, or biscuit, and the words Mum and Dad didn't seem to have an ending. The only reason he could say ASDA was because of repetition and he loved the advert. Move on 12 months, and I've given up work, and Robert is in mainstream nursery where they placed him on their SEN register within his first 6 months! This was the start of a very long journey for us.

M: What age was Robert diagnosed with Asperger's?

By the time Robert was six, we had an Asperger's diagnosis with a specific learning difficulty—dyslexia, and by the time he was nine we had added ADHD to the list.

I was a mother bear possessed at the beginning! I was not going to let this beat us. I was going to fight, scream, and get results, whatever it took! What I didn't do too well was the bereavement, grieving for the child I could have had, and all the emotions that are tied up in that one word. That train crash happened sometime later, between the end of one fight, and the beginning of another!

It wasn't until we found out about our son's autism diagnosis that I realised my husband could be in that camp too! It answered so many questions within our relationship; how he dealt with social interaction, and so many other awkward situations, his obsession with having enough money, and not being in any kind of debt, which could be completely irrational sometimes. Other people just couldn't understand why we were still together! I knew somewhere there would be answers. I found them when autism came crashing headlong into our lives.

M: How did the school respond?

Robert attended mainstream school, and was on school action during nursery, and school action plus from Reception until his Statement of Education issued 2005. During the interim period—before statutory assessment—Robert was such a handful that a teaching assistant, who was already supporting a child with Statement in the class, helped him too. Personally, it was not an arrangement we were happy with; apart from taking up time from another child, we felt they were using it as an excuse not to fully address Robert's needs. I was told by school that the only way I could possibly *speed this up,* was to put in a parental request. I had no idea where to start, and was really left to my own devices. No clear signposting or direction given at all. The school agreed to support the request, but to be quite honest, I don't think they really wanted to engage with the actual doing bit! I wanted everyone singing from the same hymn sheet, so to ensure this was going to happen, I knew I would have to take the lead on this. Scary is an understatement, I knew my son's education, and life depended on me making the right choices. Many professionals came to *make observations* of Robert, and had plenty to say about him, but nobody was actually making a decision. I had a really good dialogue with the school; I think having an older child there helped as relationships with staff had already been established. I started to get slightly paranoid being called in after school almost every day though. I just knew what was coming when the door opened and the hand beckoned! I think I spent years mastering the art of rolling my eyes! During my search, I stumbled across the local Parent Partnership Manager, she was a godsend and I would strongly recommend any parents in the process to seek out their local Parent Partnership Officer. She really helped us when we had to appeal against the decision *not* to assess, and we managed to turn it around. For Jonathan and I, the whole process was about us leading the way; pushing, and basically getting on their nerves to get results. It was physically tiring to say the least, but we decided that we wanted Robert to experience everything that Elizabeth had; we wanted to give him chances like all the other children were given. We were quite prepared to do absolutely anything to give him those opportunities. Someone once told me to never wrap him up in cotton wool, that the world will never be that fluffy! I've always stuck by that. If I don't let him dip his toe into the sea of life, how will he know what it feels like!

M: Food fads in teenagers are bad enough, but around your dinner table, they're slightly more challenging, aren't they?

Food and the art of eating has always been a contentious issue in our house, long before the children came along. Before I had my epiphany about my hubby, and his undiagnosed Asperger's, I used to think his attitude about food was incredibly unreasonable at times, spoilt, snooty, and downright stubborn. When I presented him with a home-cooked spaghetti bolognese, and he would only eat the bol, I really did become quite paranoid. He would claim that the pasta was like eating slugs—all slimy—and I often thought this was quite simply an exaggeration. So many times he used to remove himself from the dining table because the noise of crunchy carrots was like someone running nails down a blackboard, or the over dramatic outbursts at the prospect of crisp packets rustling whilst watching films. The rigidity, and inability to compromise, was so frustrating to me and a dispute would go on for days. I had been brought up with the attitude you eat whatever was put on your plate or go hungry! I wasn't very sympathetic. That was until I had children.

Easy job with my daughter, she would try anything, hardly any resistance, and loved her veg! I became quite complacent when Robert came along, that was until I stopped breastfeeding, and tried to bottle feed him. Ewww, icky baby! Projectile everything—and I mean everything, everywhere—I didn't know one small baby could hold so much. He must have been holding onto more than his own body weight. Poor mite, he suffered dreadfully with eczema, and asthma, and ended up only tolerating baby soya milk. By the time he had reached solids and beyond, we had a limited palate of taste—Weetabix or Ready Brek, chicken nuggets, loved the taste of fromage frais, though we had to be careful not too many, raw carrots if we were lucky, bread and butter, sultanas (they were sweets), and if we were in the mood, mashed potato. Over time we have added to our list, but we are not experimental, and have been influenced by hubby's own food issues.

Robert's sensory issues include food smells—that's tricky to deal with when you're 30,000 ft in an airplane and he's screaming he wants to get off! Robert can't abide anybody eating in close proximity, so eats on his own, even on Xmas day! We don't seem to have an *off* button either, so the consumption of a treat, biscuits say, can go on until we have eaten the entire packet in one sitting. Quite recently, I entered the dark hole that is Robert's room only to find the empty 500g packet of sultanas hidden under his pillow. I'd only bought them the day before! I have tried to ask him why he does it, but he gets agitated with me, so I've just accepted it's one of his *things,* and I will just have to watch him more carefully.

Robert's medication for ADHD doesn't help; it suppresses appetite, so when it's worn off he's got the munchies. I cook most meals from scratch because I'm fully aware of the necessity of five a day, but it's tricky when you have a child who has so many issues with food. Until you start to really think about it, you don't pay much attention to how much these issues control your lives.

M: You've had a lot of involvement with your local SEN Parents Forum. Has the contact with other parents helped?

In my quest for SEN knowledge, and a keen interest in meeting other parents locally, I joined the Parents Forum three years ago. Initially, I went along just to find out what was going on in our local authority as most of you are familiar with local authorities *really* don't like SEN parents getting to know too much! Crikey, if we knew too much we might see more clearly their short comings! Through the meetings I became aware that I did have more to contribute than I first thought. I'd spent years trapped in this emotional bubble, and trying to find that even keel, trying desperately to balance that see-saw of our life, that I lost sight of who I was, and who I had worked hard to be. What I found confusing too, was realising that who you want to be is an ever evolving situation. That can be unnerving, a little bit scary, and I was treading uncharted territory. Could I possibly have anything to give or share? Do you know, and I can say this now: *Yes I do*!

I'm really passionate about SEN parents and their capacity as an entity, a united voice to influence change. I've participated as a Parent Rep on local authority task and finish groups, third party steering groups, and parent led visioning events. I started off being very conservative, and reserved, taking a more secure position of just nodding and listening. I was struggling inside to have that inner confidence that:

1. I had anything relevant to say.
2. That I would be heard.

Stepping over that line came as a bit of a shock to me. I'd had a really crappy week with Robert's anxiety, and was truly fed up with the attitude of some people, so when asked whether parents might engage with a new process, I just let rip! Not in a naughty way, or angry outburst kind of way. I merely pointed out quite honestly, and calmly, the impact of continual assessments, the tiresomeness of repeating your child's history to half a dozen practitioners and the endless filling out of forms, etc., etc.

I tried to convey what it's truly like on the front line for SEN parents, warts and all! Letting them know we don't want pity. We want answers. We want compromises. We want choices, and most of all, we want respect, and a voice in the decision making of our children's futures. Shocked? You bet I was, more so because they all listened! I wouldn't say now I have a Rottweiler reputation per sé, but I don't hold back and will ask squirmy questions. Parents want to be able to make informed choices and that's not too much to ask.

So now I just love these sessions at the local parents forum. They get you fired up, enthused, and above all made me realise that goals are attainable.

Oh, and did I mention that recently I was voted Chair Person? And to think I started off as a wallflower.

M: How do you cope with the meltdowns?

Meltdowns are the times that the complexities of having

high functioning autism, and ADHD, are brought home, and I am reminded of the internal war my son suffers. Initially, we were told Robert had semantic pragmatic disorder, and I scoured the internet to find out as much information as I could. I was like a dog with a bone. I had to do something, didn't know what, but something. My emotions were trying to creep out of the suitcase, and the more I researched, the more power I had to push them back in there. In my mind, I was charging right up to the gate, hammering on it, slapping my chest, then gesturing with my hands "C'mon bring it on!" just like the gangster films. Only if I'd known then, what I know now, I would have saved that one for later. I used to sit in the dark with only the light of the computer screen illuminating my tear sodden face, because the more I read, the more I realised that this wasn't just a blip in our speech and language development, whatever it was, it was going to be life-changing. You are all probably wondering where my husband, Jonathan was? I'm sure this will resonate with some of you out there; the bucket of sand was more inviting! I knew my journey for knowledge, or anything else relating to our children, was going to be a solitary one.

Within 2 years we had gone through semantic pragmatic disorder, autistic spectrum disorder, and then to Asperger's, and our specific learning difficulty—dyslexia thrown in for good measure. By the time Robert was 9 we managed to add ADHD and the diagnosing Consultant decided because Robert had developmental delay in speech it was not Asperger's but high functioning autism. Confusing to say the least, but my dog and bone attitude meant that the acquisition of information at the time was top priority. I had to get my head round it all so I could help Robert.

Not that I was much help yesterday. The incident was

simple—last lesson of the day, one child winding up Robert, questioning about friendship with a girl (who I might add has been one of two friends he has had since the beginning of secondary school that *get him*), Robert does not want to answer (because you just don't!), pick, pick, pick, throw a piece of Lego at him and *BOOM*! Mum arrives and we start. We go on about how it's always him they pick on—nobody listens—it's not fair—nobody punishes other people's bad behaviour—he always gets the blame, and then for the real cruncher,

"It's all you and Dad's fault I have this autism and ADHD. You're the ones who gave me this cell. ADHD won't let my brain calm down." And "Autism and ADHD stops me from fighting my own battles"…and he went on, and on, and on.

I try the calm approach, trying to reassure, trying to remind him about the discussion we had about other people, and how they treat us, and that some children find that once they get a reaction from you, feel that they can do it time and time again, but more importantly, how do we control the situation when this happens? I pulled out everything from my mummy armoury. Could I comfort my boy? Not a cat in hells chance!

I was driving while this was happening, heading for the motorway for a little diversion; I hoped it would work because I was running out of ideas! I told Robert firmly that the conversation would have to stop because I was driving, and if I tried to concentrate on his issues and drive at the same time I would have an accident. Ah, silence!! The rule card played off.

I took him to a shop. Many will say not a bright move because we don't do supermarkets, but it worked. We bought our items, we grabbed a coke and some fries, went to get in the car, and this young man walking out with me says

81

"Mum, I think I've calmed down now. It's my ADHD that makes me do that. I think my outburst was because it was the end of the day, and my tablet had worn off."

I found myself having a moment…my goodness, I never thought the day would arrive when my boy would be able to make a complex analysis of his own behaviour, and attribute it to his condition.

My word, Robert has started his journey into transition. Now Robert is a bright, caring, and sometimes surprising young teen. We have days that are not so good, some that are different, and some days that are more autistic than ADHD. We are sailing headlong into adulthood transition, which is challenging to say the least, and if I had known back at the beginning of our journey what I do now I would have started my blog sooner.

Saying that, you can only start something when you are in the right place, and we've come a long way to be in that right place, documenting it seemed the obvious next step.

I try to write about Robert with humour, sense of hope, and positivity. I hope I achieve that. In our house there is no room for negativity; we don't have enough time!

Jo Worgan

"**I** knew something was *not right* before Tom's first birthday. There were lots of different things that niggled me, and I kept thinking, something is wrong with this child, but I didn't know what. By Tom's second birthday I definitely knew. He would scream, and shout, and have meltdowns for no reason. He would flap his hands, and be very active and unsettled. He would not use a fork or spoon, and he seemed to regress with both language and diet."

Jo's Journey

I was born in Birkenhead, on the Wirral, in northern England in 1975. Then, when I was nine, we moved a few miles away to Moreton.

I'm the eldest of four: two girls, then two boys. I had an extremely happy childhood with lots of days out and family time together. I was the sensible older sister, and when my youngest brother was born, I was 13 and acted as a second mum really. I loved looking after him though.

M: What was your first job after leaving school?

I went straight to university to study English Literature and Drama with Theatre Studies and I gained a BA (Hons) in 1996. While studying, I also worked a night shift once a week at a nursing home, which I loved, and where my mum also worked. Once I had finished my degree I wanted to do my teacher training but I found it very difficult to access a PGCE course as I had a combined honours degree. So I decided to have a complete change, and I went and got a job as a dental nurse, and worked at the same practice until 2000 which was when I left to start my nurse training.

M: What made you decide to go into nursing?

My mum has always done care work, and she herself was a state enrolled nurse. I also enjoyed my work as a care assistant at the nursing home so I thought why not go and train as a nurse. I love looking after people so I thought why not give it a go.

M: Where did you do nurse's training, and why specialise in renal nursing?

I trained at Arrow Park Hospital in Upton through Chester University. My intake was the last one as a school of nursing based in the hospital. We had no lectures in the university as the whole three year course was hospital based. I loved it, and gained a diploma in higher education with Registered General Nurse status. During the last three months of training you could choose a specialism, and I chose renal nursing as I thought it seemed interesting. I remember my first day on the haemodialysis unit. I was scared to death, all the machines were beeping, and tubes everywhere, but after a few weeks I loved it. The unit where I was working was only a satellite unit, the main unit being at the Royal Liverpool hospital, and me being the cheeky person that I was, and still am, I asked to go and have a placement over there. Somehow they agreed to this, and while working there they offered me a job as a newly qualified nurse. I was there for a total of 6 months as we had to relocate to Dorset for my husband's new job. Luckily though, I managed to find bank work at the hospital in Dorchester, and for 6 months I worked on surgery, orthopaedics, and elderly care. This was all fantastic experience, but I kept popping into the dialysis unit, and when a vacancy became available, I got the job. So I then worked on the haemodialysis unit, general ward, and peritoneal dialysis outreach team. I also completed my renal course so that I became a senior renal nurse within the unit.

M: Tell us about your family?

I met my husband Andrew at school when we were both 15. We are the same age, and I knew the moment I saw him that we would get married one day. We were chatting one evening when we were 18 and Andrew said, "Shall we get married?" And I said, "okay." We have been together ever since. Andrew went to Bangor University to study marine chemistry, and he stayed 4 years as he did his master's degree there. When he came back home to the Wirral, I was working as a dental nurse, and he started his Ph.D. at Liverpool John Moores University. It took him 6 years as he was working as a lab technician at the same time, but it enabled us to save money, and get our first mortgage and home.

We married on the 20th June 1998. It was a church wedding, I wore a white dress, and we had a buffet, and disco afterwards in a local pub, so a very cheap wedding, but such a lovely day with all of our family and friends.

We have two sons: Stephen is 6½; he was born on the

30th November 2006, in Dorset by emergency c section, long story. He was 16 months old when Tom was born on 8th April 2008, in Lancaster, also by emergency c section, another long story. They are both very special and unique.

Tom is five and he goes to Hillside Specialist School for children with autism spectrum disorders, it is in Longridge, Preston. He did one term at mainstream school with one-to-one support but this did not work out as he needs specialist interventions. He started at Hillside in Jan 2013. This was the best decision I ever made. Tom is a  character, he is very blunt and straight to the point, takes everything literally, so you have to watch what you say. He struggles in social situations with sharing, communication, and social rules, but we muddle through, he also has very little sense of danger, and has to be watched constantly, I am forever on my guard. Times at home can be very difficult in trying to keep the peace. He loves books, stories, his IPad, computer, DS, play dough, and playfoam. He loves to lie on the floor surrounded by his cars. He loves outdoors, and enjoys the garden slide and trampoline. He also loves to go to the farm and playground. He can be very caring, and shows empathy if someone is hurt or upset. He is very tactile, and enjoys massage, and strokes to his back and legs/feet. He benefits from a visual timetable, and simple instructions. He can be very funny, and makes me laugh. He can also be very aggressive though, and hit out and shout, but this is usually short lived, and soon forgotten.

Stephen is 6½ and the big brother. He is so very caring, and rather a sensitive soul. He is very protective of Tom and very understanding. He has an amazing imagination, and acts out either being a palaeontologist, or a Jedi knight, or an Eddie Stobart trucker. He wants to be a palaeontologist when he is older, but he does not want to go to university as it will be boring. He loves to read, he reads very well. He also loves to tell me stories that he has made up. He really enjoys swimming with his dad, and like Tom, enjoys being outdoors. We try to make time for Stephen of a weekend, and in the holidays. It is one of the reasons that I put Tom into holiday club as we get time alone with him. I do worry that Stephen feels he has to care for Tom, and therefore I feel that he needs time just for him to be a little boy. We often have treat nights where we either watch dinosaur movies, or Eddie Stobart. He is a very special little boy.

They are both so very different, and although they can argue as brothers do, they are very fond of each other, and call each other best friend.

M: When did you first have concerns about Tom's development?

I knew something was *not right* before Tom's first birthday. There were lots of different things that niggled me really, and I kept thinking, something is wrong with this child but I didn't know what. By his second birthday I definitely knew. He would scream, and shout, and have meltdowns for no reason. He would flap his hands, and be very active, and unsettled. He would not use a fork or spoon, and he seemed to regress with both language, and diet. He also started to want things to be the same, to eat the same foods, do things the same way, put clothes on in the same order, and go the same routes when out and about. He would also not settle for anyone else other than me, when he started nursery at age 2, after a month a meeting was called in which the nursery voiced their concerns regarding Toms behaviour. He would not settle, would not share, and was very much doing things on his own agenda, he would not follow simple instructions. This was how he was at home.

M: Had you had much contact with children on the autistic spectrum?

I knew very little about autism, and had never met any children on the autistic spectrum prior to receiving help and support. Once I started to receive help from the children's centre, I started to go to the peer support group there, AOK, which support families who have children with additional needs, with or without, diagnosis. It was here that I met many parents, and their children, I still go today. This completely changed my life, I met inspirational parents who gave me wonderful advice, and support, and over the years I have been able to do the same.

M: Although Tom's diagnosis must have been difficult to come to terms with, was it a relief to have your suspicions confirmed?

I always knew something was different about him, and when I started to receive support, I started investigating, I always had in the back of my mind that he was autistic, and it was only when my mum asked me what I thought was wrong, that I voiced this. When looking on the National Autistic Society website I then knew that Tom was on the autistic spectrum. Over several appointments with the paediatrician she gave us a diagnosis of: ASD (autistic spectrum disorder), then probable ASD, then ASD. So this happened gradually for us. Although it came as no surprise, I did feel relief that he had been diagnosed, and that this opened up the door for more help, and services. However, strangely I also felt deep sadness and guilt, that somehow I was to blame, and that yes, he is autistic. There was now no doubt.

My advice now, with hindsight, is that if you have concerns, talk to your Health Visitor, for children under five, and also contact your local children's centre for advice, and support. I did not know this at the time, and it was only because the nursery was based at the children's centre that we received help.

M: What has been the biggest challenge in dealing with Tom's disability?

I can cope with most things really, you learn to adapt to the challenges you are faced with at both home and out and about. This is within my control. However, the biggest challenge that I have been faced with so far is with regards to his education, and in getting him correctly placed in an autism specific specialist school. Although I was included in the process of gaining a statement, I felt that my wishes, and concerns about placing Tom into a mainstream setting were not listened to. However he is now where he needs to be, and progressing well.

M: What I found particularly interesting about your book, *My life With Tom*, was the transition from nursery to mainstream class, and then to a specialised school—

and all before the age of six. For any parent with a young child on the spectrum, your journey must give them much hope as to what can be achieved with the appropriate education. Sadly though, it seems these specialised schools are few and far between, and the outside looking in situation you found yourself and Tom in during the short spell at mainstream school is a sad reality for a lot of children and parents today. To place a child in a mainstream school setting, that they may have an adverse reaction to seems counter-productive, and must be heart-wrenching for the parents. I wonder, why it is not a legal requirement for every county to provide a specialised school for children, and young people with ASD?

Tom attended a mainstream school for one term, and it was a total disaster. This was through no fault of the school's. They did their very best in giving Tom one-to-one support from the very beginning, even without a correct statement of educational needs to being in place. Tom was only given part-time support, and it was agreed with the school that he needed full-time support. He needed help with dressing, his personal care needs (he was and still is in nappies), his associated sensory needs, and challenging behaviours, his lack of danger, as well as his entire specific educational needs due to his ASD. However, the truth was, it was not the correct environment for him to be in. The class size was far too large; 38 children in total, the classroom had all the typical drawings, and artwork hanging from the ceiling, and it was small, so this created lots of sensory overload for Tom. There was also no safe play area for Tom as the school gates were not locked and secure, so when outside during morning play, he only accessed at most two hours of school during the morning, he had to hold onto his Teaching Assistant's hand.

During this time I had very close contact with the school, and the Head teacher, I have to say, was very supportive in getting Tom into the right setting for his needs. Together with the local education authority, a specialist ASD school was found, albeit in the next county, a forty-five minute drive away, where he travels on the school bus with an escort. Tom went from a class of 38 children, to a class of 9. He was able to access safe outside play, a soft play room, and a sensory room. The whole school environment was catered to meet his needs.

Although both upsetting for myself and Tom, I know that we have been extremely lucky. Tom was given a statement of educational needs. Although I had to fight initially to get the correct level of support for him, in the end he did receive it. For many parents this is the first battle on the rocky educational journey for their child. I also feel that Tom was very quickly placed into a specialist ASD school, and I know many other parents whose child should be placed in a similar setting, but due to lack of places, funding, or diagnosis, many children who are on the higher level of the spectrum find it increasingly difficult to access specialist provision, this is not possible. Therefore I am eternally grateful that Tom is where he is.

M: Do you worry about the future?

I worry all the time about his future, it is very early days for Tom, and we do not know how he will progress, but it is always at the back of my mind, "who will look after Tom when I am no longer here?" I am unsure at the moment if Tom will be able to lead an independent life, or if he will need some sort of support, I just don't know. The future is a very uncertain one for him, and that does frighten me. I also worry about how vulnerable he will be out there because of his disability, and that he may become the target of bullying. I worry all the time, although I try not to.

This was very much brought home to me by an incident that happened on a bus ride home with the boys. We were sat at the back of the bus, and Tom became very distressed, and had an autistic meltdown, I had to try, and keep him safe, as well as trying to calm him down, difficult on a busy, moving bus. While doing so, I was verbally attacked by a fellow passenger who told me to "control my child as he was disturbing the other passengers." When I tried to explain to her that he was autistic, and could not control his behaviour, she launched into an attack of how autism does not exist, and that it is "just a label used as an excuse for naughty children." This is what I fear, that Tom will not be understood, he will be so very vulnerable, and subjected to bigoted, and uneducated opinions such as this passenger's. The future, I feel, is a very frightening one.

This is why I support Kevin Healey, and his Autism Anti-Bullying Campaign, I want Tom to be better protected, and supported as an adult who is on the autistic spectrum, as we do with all of our children.

M: We have both found an outlet in writing, and thanks to the internet, there are no geographical boundaries, so we've been able to share our stories with people from all over the world. Tell us about your books.

I started to write *Life on the Spectrum: The Preschool Years, Getting the Help and Support You Need,* in the summer of 2012. I sat one day with Tom on my knee, and I just thought how lucky, and well supported we had been in getting a diagnosis, and interventions for Tom. I felt incredibly sad for those parents who were not so lucky. I thought to myself, why not write a book about the help, and support we received, just telling our story, but at the same time giving lots of practical information and resources. So I did. I sat and wrote the whole book on my iPhone, usually with Tom draped all over me. I honestly thought that only a handful of people would read it, and was genuinely surprised when I received comments from parents from all over the world. I also enjoyed writing the book, it was very cathartic for me, and in a way I felt that I could move on.

I started writing a blog after I had published *Life on the Spectrum*. I still felt the need to write, and in a way I needed to vent my feelings, frustrations, and celebrations. By doing so I also connected to many other parent bloggers, and gained much support. It was when talking to my Auntie one day, on the phone, that she suggested I put all my blogs into a book, and I thought, why not? Sounds like a good idea, and so I did. It is another way to reach out and support other parents in similar situations, as well as being a lovely keepsake for me, of life with my boys when they were little.

M: Now that the children are in school, have you taken up any special interests?

I decided that once Tom was settled in school, that I would go and volunteer at the local village preschool. This was where Tom attended. I contacted the local further education college, and they agreed that I could start my level 3 once I had my placement. So I started my NVQ level 3 in Children's and Young People's Workforce in February this year. I volunteer for a couple of days a week and I really enjoy it. I needed something to do, to get me out of the house, and to just be me, rather than Tom's mum. I cannot go back to work at the moment so this is ideal for me. I will have finished the course by October.

M: I'd like to finish with a few lines from your book, *My Life with Tom*. What you say must resonate with parents of special needs children the world over…

My Tom is four and has autistic spectrum disorder. There are many comments when people meet him, including:

"He doesn't look autistic."

"How awful for you."

"I am so sorry."

Although people do not mean to inflict hurt with their words, they do.

So here is the truth.

Autism is a *hidden* developmental disability, which affects the person socially, behaviourally, and communicatively. Above all though, he is my little boy. He does not *look* autistic, I do not think life is *awful*, and I am not sorry that I have him in my life. He makes life special.

M: Amen.

Julia Donal

"**From** nowhere, the screams of my 11-year-old son, Tony, pierced the bright, sunny afternoon. As I turned, he was running towards me with his arms out-stretched, eyes bulging with terror. "Mum-Mum-come-quick, our Cathy's been run over!" My heart was racing, pounding, as we both ran frantically back toward the road where a crowd of people were already gathered. I pushed my way through, and couldn't believe what I saw before me. My six-year-old daughter, my beautiful little girl, was lying in the middle of the road. Blood was coming out of her nose, and her ear, her leg was bent halfway up her back, and her eyes were tightly shut.

I thought she was dead."

Julia's Journey

CATHERINE

There's a little girl who stayed when Alice came back home

And there's a small child in wonderland alone

She didn't mean to go away

She only left the house to play

And now she sits in silence

Sleeping in the stars at night in golden slumber

breathing light

A lean gazelle that's taken fright,

afraid, to come back home.

Written by Catherine's brother, Tony

M: Julia, I can't imagine what you went through when you saw your little girl lying in the road. It sounds like every parent's worst nightmare.

I wished it was a nightmare I could wake from, but sadly, it was all very real. Only two hours earlier I'd held my little Catherine's hand, and walked her back to school after lunch. She'd chattered away to me, and when we reached the school gate she ran inside to her friends, then turned to wave at me. If only I'd known when she waved goodbye from the playground that day, shouting "Bye Mum, see you after," that it would be the last time she would ever talk to me; that she would be hit by a lorry on her way home from school, and left with severe brain damage.

That day I bent down to where she lay in the road, I was about to take her in my arms when I was restrained by some of the parents at the scene. A woman I didn't recognise looked at me pitifully and said it was best not to touch her. I tried to fight them off but my arms were being held so firmly that I couldn't move them. I dropped my head in despair, and sobbed as I looked at the body of my baby lying helpless, and injured on the road.

And then the sound of the siren brought me to my senses as the ambulance arrived, and my caring captors released me. Two paramedics jumped from the ambulance, opened the back doors, and brought out a stretcher. I watched them crouch down on the tarmac and gently place the lifeless body of my little girl upon it. It was so awful. I followed them into the back of the ambulance as they placed her on the narrow bed, the doors slammed shut, and we sped away.

The emergency siren blasted all the way to the hospital, shooting through red lights in order to save my daughter's life. I knelt down beside her on the ambulance floor and held her tiny hand, praying that she wouldn't die; God, how I prayed that day, and many more days after.

When we arrived at the hospital, a medical team had been standing by to meet us. Gentle hands transferred Catherine onto a trolley and my little girl was quickly rushed into an examination room.

They wouldn't let me go with her. No matter how much I begged and pleaded, they wouldn't let me follow. I was frantic. I was shown into a waiting room where I sat alone with my head in my hands, out of my mind with worry. It was a while later that I heard my husband's voice asking where Catherine and I were. The nurse brought him to me and we just looked at one another, too grief stricken to speak. He walked towards me and we held each other tight, united in the fear and uncertainty of whether our beautiful daughter was going to live or die.

Soon a doctor came into the room and gave us his diagnosis. He said that Catherine had suffered multiple and appalling injuries. Her condition was very serious and they would have to operate straight away.

So we waited, and waited, and the hours sped by. The longer we waited the more anxious we became. Then at last—it was about eight o'clock in the evening when the doctor came into the room. We could tell by the look on his face that it wasn't good news.

"I'm afraid your daughter's condition is very serious", he said sympathetically. "She has suffered severe head injuries resulting in irreparable damage to her brain. The femur in her right leg is broken, and all we can do now is make her as comfortable as possible. She may not survive the night, but if she does, the next 24 hours will be crucial. I suggest that you inform the rest of your family. I'm sure they would like to see her."

I remember staring at him. I couldn't believe what he was saying. He said that our bright, mischievous little girl was probably going to die. But he didn't know her like we did. I thought he must have been mistaken. I mean, doctors always paint things darker than they really are. "No! No! No!" I screamed. "You're wrong. I don't believe you!"

Just then a staff nurse came into the room with a small glass of water and a white tablet. She offered them to me and said "Please, please take this. It will help you. You'll be going to see Catherine soon, and I'm sure she wouldn't like to see her mum so upset." I told the nurse I didn't want any drugs. I didn't want to be put to sleep. I just wanted to see my little girl. She assured me the tablet wouldn't put me to sleep; it would just calm my nerves, so I took it.

M: You must have been desperate to see Catherine and hold her in your arms.

Oh, I'll never forget when we first saw her. Catherine's father and I stood on either side of her bed in complete silence. The tiny figure on the bed looked nothing like our daughter. Her bandaged head seemed to have swollen to twice its natural size. Her forehead and eyelids were black and blue; her very swollen leg was in an iron cast. I reached down and clutched her tiny hand in mine. Her father was leaning on the bed with his head bowed, silently sobbing. We were in utter despair—our daughter was going to die, and there was nothing we could do about it.

M: How on earth had it happened?

If only we could turn back the clock.

A split second was all it had taken.

I had agreed to allow Catherine to walk home with her friends because I knew there was a lollipop man in attendance so I knew that she would be in safe hands. We learnt that day that as Catherine was being crossed over the carriageway by the lollipop man, and whilst she stood in the grassy area of the middle section with the other children waiting to be safely led across, excitement at seeing a familiar face on the other side of the road had erased all caution as she broke away from the group of youngsters and ran across to greet them.

Catherine (right) and Julianne, before the accident

M: You had other children you had to think about too, didn't you?

Catherine was the youngest of four, with two older sisters and a brother. My eldest daughter, Christine, was thirteen-years-old, my son Tony was eleven, and my daughter Julianne was eight. Catherine had just had her sixth birthday the week before. Neighbours jumped to our rescue and took them in that day. I knew they would all be watching out the window, noses pressed to the glass, waiting for our return. You know how hopeful children are. They'd be expecting us to walk through the door any minute with Catherine, having nothing more than a bandaged leg.

After an hour or so of sitting beside Catherine's hospital bed, the ward sister said it might be a good idea if my husband and I went home and told Catherine's brother and sister's how ill their little sister was. We couldn't leave her side. The doctor told us our baby girl could die during the night, but she assured us that Catherine would be in safe hands. We left the hospital in a daze and got a taxi outside.

We were eager to see our children, but not looking forward to what we had to tell them. What could we tell them? Certainly not the truth about how serious their sister's injuries were.

We arrived home and told the children that we all had to pray very hard. It was with a heavy heart that we kissed them goodnight and sent them off to bed.

M: That must have been a long night for you?

We couldn't go to bed; sleep was impossible. We had no phone but rang throughout the night from a public call-box on the corner of our street. I prayed the police wouldn't knock on our door. We wouldn't even need to open it, would we? Their presence could only mean one thing.

My husband rang the hospital before we left and was told by the ward sister that Catherine had deteriorated and her condition was critical. When we arrived at the hospital, the doctor said that Catherine had been taken off the breathing machine, but that was all she could do. Her condition was critical and could turn fatal at any time. She had slipped into a coma, which could last days weeks even months. We were devastated.

The next day I was in a trance as I got the children ready for school. As soon as they left I got the bus down to the hospital. It was a long thirty minutes.

There was still no change. Catherine had a feeding tube through her nose and I was longing to lift her into my arms but we could only hold her hand and speak to her through our tears.

After our tears subsided—although there were many more to come—Catherine's father and I had to decide what

103

we were going to do. There was no way we could leave
Catherine on her own while she was in a coma; one of us
would have to be there talk to her, and let her know we
were right beside her. However, we had three other children at home who needed us, and they were suffering as
well. We were a unit of six and one was missing, so we
were incomplete. We decided that I would stay with Catherine in the daytime and be home for my children coming
home from school, and her father would call in to see her
on his way home from work. That way one of us would be
there if worst came to worst.

M: It's said, if God takes us to it, then God sees us
through it, but I don't know how I would have coped
with all you had to bear.

Looking back, I don't know how I got through it. I remember a few days after the accident getting off the bus a stop
before the hospital and going into the Catholic Church.
To the right of me, just inside a small alcove, there stood
a statue of St. Jude; my aunt always told me he was the pa-
tron saint of lost causes, so I knelt on the tiny wooden support, clasped my hands, and prayed; God, how I prayed.
I begged St. Jude to ask God to spare Catherine; to let her
live. "We don't care what's wrong with her." I whispered.
"We will always look after her—just please, please—don't
let her die."

I left the church and took the short walk to the hospital, hoping against all hope that a miracle had occurred.
I thought I would walk into the ward and my husband,
Tony, would be standing there with a big smile on his face
and he'd say, "Catherine's awake! She's awake, and asking
for you." Then Catherine would look at me and say, "Hiya
Mum, when can I come home?" I hurried into the building and towards the ward. I couldn't wait to see her. When

she comes home, I thought, I'll take her to the cake shop and buy her the biggest custard tart she has ever seen, because that was her favourite. But of course I'd let my imagination run away with me. When I reached my daughter's bed she was lying in the same position, on her back, with her eyes tightly closed.

The hospital gave us a parent's room, which consisted of basic essentials, two single beds, and facilities to make a cup of tea but we really didn't bother with it because we were both too anxious to relax.

One month went by, then two, and three, and four. I went to the hospital every afternoon, always making sure I was home for the children when they returned from school. There was never any improvement; Catherine was still in a coma.

M: You must have been emotionally, and financially drained.

We were. I had to leave my part-time job and my husband lost his job because of the time he had to take off work, so we were hit from all sides. But just when we thought we'd hit rock bottom, and were totally and utterly burnt out, we walked onto the ward one day—Catherine had been in a coma for six months—and my heart started pounding when I saw the ward sister and priest standing at Catherine's bed. We hurried towards them only to be met with a beaming smile.

"Look" the ward sister said, "she's coming out of her coma!"

Catherine's father and I looked at one another in disbelief, our faces must have glowed with happiness. We were elated, and so full of joy; I thought I was going to burst.

The doctor walked briskly into the ward, eager to see his little patient. He stood at the foot of her bed, then he smiled and said, "Hello Catherine, how are you? It's lovely to see you!" She stared at him blankly. He examined her and said "She's in a comatose condition at the moment. The best thing to do is talk to her, and keep talking to her, as you've been doing all this time. I'll arrange for a specialist to come and do an assessment".

We sat on either side of Catherine's bed and held her hand. She looked at us with a vacant stare. At that moment we didn't care what she could or could not do. She had been so ill—what did we expect?

When we went home and told the kids the news they were so excited asking when their baby sister could home. I told them what the doctor told us, that before she could come home she would have to be seen by a specialist and that wouldn't be until after Christmas.

I will never forget that glorious day—the day she came out of the coma—it was the 19th December

We didn't mind waiting to bring her home. We'd already waited six agonising months for this day

On Christmas Day, Christine, young Tony, Julianne, her father, and I all sat around Catherine's bed. As each of us spoke to her she just looked at us with no sign of recognition; she just lay there, propped up with pillows.

When the nurse came to change her there were no signs of protest, her arms and legs just flopped like a rag doll. Still, for all she had been through, she was a picture of beauty. Her dark thick hair curled around her face. Her eyes, though dull, were tinted green, and her skin was lovely and pink. She was indeed, though awake, a sleeping beauty.

The New Year began, and there was no great improvement in Catherine's condition. She still had to have a feed tube inserted through her nose because she was unable to swallow. I hated it and told the ward sister so, but she smiled and said that I needed to learn how to insert it before Catherine came home. That made me nervous, and she assured me a district nurse would call four times a week to give me help and support, which made me feel better.

M: How was Catherine's assessment with the paediatrician?

Catherine's assessment was on 5th February 1973. The day we met the specialist (paediatric neurologist) is another experience etched in my mind.

We got to the hospital early, and waited anxiously for his arrival. He walked into the ward and approached Catherine's bed, acknowledging my husband and I with a nod of the head. Then he pursed his lips together, and stood for a while at the bottom of our daughter's bed looking at her, and then, at last, he proceeded to examine her.

We stood quietly as he looked deep into her eyes with his special torch. When he pinched her hands and feet she moved slightly. He examined her chest, and looked into her ears.

As he straightened himself up, he sighed deeply, and shook his head from side to side; then he looked at her father and I and said coldly: "The best advice that I can give you both is to go home and take care of the three children you have. The kindest thing you can do for this child is to have her placed in some kind of care home and let someone else take care of her. She will never be able to do anything for herself, and will always have to depend on someone. She will never walk, talk, or be able to feed herself. All in all, she will be totally dependent on others for the rest of her life. She will always be in nappies and as far as the quality of her life is concerned—it will be non-existent."

Her father and I were shocked. It wasn't about the assessment results; it was his cold and condescending attitude—and the way he'd spoken about Catherine.

M: I think he was right to offer you a choice; an option to walk away from the long uncertain road you were about to embark on. There may well have been some that would have taken that advice, but I agree, it was the delivery of the information that was so hurtful. How did you respond to him?

My husband stared at the doctor, I could see his fists were clenched. I put my hand on his arm to restrain him and said quietly. "We're not going to take any notice of him. Just wait till we get her back home, we'll get her better; just wait and see." Then the specialist picked up his brief case from the chair, nodded to us and walked away.

That same day the ward sister informed us she was going to make arrangements for Catherine's return home.

M: So did that wonderful information wipe away the dark cloud the doctor had left behind him?

We were elated. Her father and I knew deep down that this was going to be an uphill struggle, but we were more than ready to take on the challenge and were going to take it day by day.

The day we brought her home in an ambulance, her father carried her into the front room and I propped her up with a couple of pillows on the settee. She was all ready and waiting for her brother and sisters when they arrived home from school. When they all came bursting in, it didn't matter that she couldn't put her arms around them; they put their arms tightly around her. They just saw her as we saw her, she was our Cathy and she was back in the fold again.

I stopped and stared at the face that looked back at me from the mirror that day; I looked so old. The stress of the last few months was beginning to take their toll. I was thirty-four years old, but I looked much older. As I turned away from the mirror, a thought occurred to me of how I was to cope with Catherine's daily needs. Then a voice seemed to say, *Do exactly what you did each time you brought a new baby home—start from the very beginning!* I felt as if a light had gone on in my head. *Thank you God, for answering my prayers!*

M: So you all managed to get back to some kind of normality. You slowly introduced Catherine to tinned baby food, and did away with her feeding tube that you so hated. But there weren't any great developments in her recovery, were there, and then two years later, as if you hadn't been through enough, your husband died in his sleep.

Yes he just couldn't cope, and found it so very difficult to accept Catherine's condition because he couldn't see any future for her. I tried to explain that her age was on her side but he still found it very difficult, and seemed to enter a world of his own—he was broken-hearted.

That was such an awful time, and I didn't know how I could ever recover from that but self pity is a luxury, I had four children who relied on me, so I carried on as best as

I could. Three years passed, and then I met a lovely man. Not everybody gets a second chance, but I did. He took on Catherine as if she was his own and he was absolutely marvellous with her, and all of my children. Bill and I married in 1980.

M: And then, together you set out on a whole new venture, didn't you?

Bill was reading the newspaper one evening and came across an article about The Institute for the Achievement of Human Potential which was based in Philadelphia and had set up The British Institute for Brain Injured Children in Somerset.

The Doman Delacato Therapy, patterns the brain into learning skills; skills that Catherine had before the accident.

The program for "brain-injured" children included:

- Patterning—manipulation of limbs and head in a rhythmic fashion
- Creeping—forward bodily movement with the abdomen in contact with the floor
- Crawling—forward bodily movement with the abdomen raised from the floor
- Receptive stimulation—visual, tactile and auditory stimulation
- Expressive activities—e.g. picking up objects
- Masking—breathing into a rebreathing mask to increase the amount of carbon dioxide inhaled, which is believed to increase cerebral blood flow
- Brachiation—swinging from a bar or vertical ladder
- Gravity/Antigravity activities—rolling, somersaulting and hanging upside down.

To be able to apply the therapy we had to have seventy volunteers, seven days a week. We approached our local parish priest, and he put us in touch with a person who was helping some young people toward achieving The Duke Of Edinburgh—so in no time at all we acquired most of our volunteers; both of our families also put their names on our rota, without them we just wouldn't have been able to do the therapy.

Catherine made really good progress. She could taste her food—her mouth had been paralyzed because she had had suffered a stroke just after the accident—she could suck through a straw, and with a little help could blow her birthday candles out.

We did the therapy from 1981 to 1985 when Catherine was turning into a young woman. She began to lose all interest in the programme so we brought it to an end.

We got on with our lives, and over the years Catherine brought us so much joy. I had my bad days, of course. The sadness would wash over me like waves, especially when the family was all together. I'd look at my grown up children, and grandchildren, and Catherine beside them, and think of all she's missed out on. Having said that, I've made sure she's lived as full a life as possible.

In 2001, Professor Tarn from Liverpool University presented Catherine with an achievement award. She had been nominated for the award by Person Shaped Support Agency (PSS), in Liverpool, who were the supporting agency at the time. Bill and I were so proud of her as she walked to the professor herself and accepted her award from him. Her father would have been proud of her too.

Catherine became a member of the Thursday Club which was a club for young people with learning difficulties. Bridge Chapel was formed by a very special lady, Lynne Lloyd, who also had a daughter with a learning disability. Lynne and her friends from Bridge Chapel bought a bungalow specifically for people with special needs, and I was delighted when Catherine was offered a place there, where she would have 24 hour support. I had just celebrated my seventieth birthday, so it made sense to accept.

M: That was a big step for all of you. How difficult was it?

I found it was very hard to cope when the time for Catherine to leave home. It was so difficult to go into her bedroom every morning to open the window as I had always done, and still do. The changes were so hard to come to terms with; two chairs at the dining table instead of three. For those first couple of weeks, I still laid three places for dinner. The worse time of course was when four o'clock came, and Catherine didn't come home from the day centre.

Over the following months, and for a long time after she'd left, I felt as if I was living in a different world. Since my other children had grown up and left home, Catherine, Bill, and I had always been together.

I bought her a new bed and furnishing for her new home because I couldn't part with any of her belongings. I felt so lost and so guilty; guilty because I just couldn't cope with her anymore.

This past June it will be forty one years since my daughter had the accident.

She has slowed down like we all do as we get older, but hasn't lost her bright and happy personality. She still has a severe learning disability, uses a wheel chair when she's out, though thankfully, she has a mobility car which her support worker drives, so her life is as full as it possibly can be. She goes shopping, bowling, and absolutely loves swimming, always accompanied by her support worker.

I ring and speak to her every morning, and every evening. I just couldn't start the day without knowing she was all right. She listens and speaks to me in her own way, with meaningful sounds and encouragement from her support worker. And she comes home for lunch twice a week, so she is still very much part of the family.

Bill and I will always be eternally grateful to The Trustees of the Bridge Chapel, in Liverpool, for providing a peaceful and secure home for Catherine. One thing I do know is that everything the trustees do, they do for the love of the Lord.

M: Come on now Julia, don't forget to tell us about your other achievements too!

Well, in the year 2000 at the grand old age of sixty, I enrolled at Liverpool Community College. Over the two years that I was there, I took English, English literature, and Creative writing and I managed to get three GCSEs.

My family was so proud, you'd have thought that I had earned a first class degree, which proves it's never too late to learn. I was fifty before I learned how to swim, so that speaks for itself doesn't it?

M: Finally, do you think you have come to terms with what happened on that awful day back in 1972?

When Catherine suffered that terrible accident, her father and I couldn't understand why. Why our little girl? We prayed so hard, and so earnestly, for her speech to be returned, but it never happened. Nevertheless, her life was spared, and we were so thankful for that. I vowed that no matter what her injuries were, we would always look after her, which we did to the best of our ability. It was too much for Catherine's father, and as time went on he just couldn't cope anymore. Looking back to that terrible day when I found him dead in his bed, I feel he was released from his torment. I will always hold a special corner in my heart just for him.

Wendy Hirst

"This last 18 months I felt as if I had my life as I knew it, taken away from me. The strokes have robbed me so much of my previous life. Now after months of being in a very dark, and dank place, I feel as though I am slowly clawing my life back. It's going to be a very long journey but if I take it one day at a time I will get there."

Wendy's Journey

I was born in Nuneaton in Warwickshire, and had a very happy childhood. I had an Italian Mother, and an English Father. My brother, Wayne, was 7 years younger than me, and life was great. Then, when I was 10, we went on holiday to Sicily to visit my maternal Grandparents and my life changed forever.

We were about 15 minutes from my Nana's village when out of nowhere a lorry did a U-turn on the motorway. There were no central barriers, and no time to stop; we hit that lorry head on. Our car was catapulted into a field at the side of the road. My brother, who was three, was killed outright as he went straight through the wind screen, and so was my cousin, and Granddad. My dad died two weeks later.

I woke up in a hospital that was very basically equipped.

116

I saw my mum in the next bed but she wouldn't speak to me. She blamed me for the accident because I changed my mind about a holiday I was going on and we all ended up going to Sicily.

I looked around for the rest of my family. I had to find my dad and my brother, but where were they?

I was told my brother was asleep in my nana's village, but of course that wasn't true because he'd been thrown through the car windscreen, and killed instantly.

Nobody would take me to find my dad, and I couldn't understand the foreign language, so I went off alone through the hospital corridor to search for him. I could hardly walk with the pain from a fractured hip, and I also had a head injury. It wasn't a long corridor, but it might as well have been 100 miles.

Somehow I managed to find my dad. I slowly opened the door to his hospital room, and certainly wasn't ready for the most heart-breaking sight I was about to see. My dad, whom I loved so much, was laid there, unable to move. In fact he looked like a neglected rag doll. He couldn't speak, hug, or even acknowledge me. I stood there and cried.

My dad now looked like a stranger, even though there was something familiar about those eyes that at one time used to sparkle. Now those eyes were dull, and virtually lifeless. I remained standing beside him in complete shock, just staring. I stayed with Dad as long as I could, then I walked slowly back to my room, the pain in my hip getting worse with each step until I fell to the floor, and was unable to get back up. Someone came, and carried me back to my bed.

I had my Italian Nana, and my English grandparents who'd flown over from England, stay with me most of the time. My brother was buried before I was out of hospital. My dad died just after I was sent home to recover at my Nana's house in the village. I found out my dad had died when my uncle came round in the early hours of the morning. I knew he had gone; I had a dream minutes before where he was sat in a tree looking down and said:

"I have to go now,
I will never leave you.
I will always be by your side."

I was unable to attend my brother's funeral, but my father's funeral was like something out of this world. My dad's coffin was carried for a mile through the streets to the church as hundreds of Italians followed to pay their respects to someone they had never met.

After the funeral service his coffin was carried from the church to the cemetery with those same people following behind. I'd never witnessed anything like it. Once we reached the cemetery my dad was laid to rest in a grave next to my brother, and my Italian Granddad. A few years later my Nana built a statue of Mary carrying Jesus over the three graves and put their photos in marble headstones.

M: That must have been a lonely journey back to England.

My dad's parents returned to England before Christmas, having stayed as long as they possibly could. My mum, Italian Nana and I, flew back home at the end of January 1980. It was snowing, and the plane was diverted, so when we landed we had to get a coach back to the midlands. I was so glad to be home, but very sad that my dad and brother weren't there with us. Walking into the house was a very emotional experience, and for years I expected my dad and brother to come through the door.

My teachers were fantastic when I returned to school a month later. It took me a while to adjust, not only because of losing Dad, my brother Wayne, Granddad and cousin, but also the amount of schooling I had missed.

I was on sleeping tablets to try and stop the nightmares, and the teachers were very understanding. However, my mother remarried within a year of my dad's passing, and her new husband made it clear he did not want a ready-made family, so I was shipped off to live with my grandparents. Shortly after I moved in with them, we moved to a seaside town in Lincolnshire for a fresh start.

M: What kind of work did you do when you left school?

When I left school there weren't that many job opportunities. I wanted to be a nursery nurse, and was a sunshine corner teacher (a church outreach) for a while.

I love children, and would play games, and share bible stories with over a 100 of them on the beach during the summer. I also became a youth leader. Then I got the chance of going to a Bible school in Scotland and jumped at it. It was the first time I had ever left home, and it was very daunting. I was the youngest there so they all used to look after me. While I was there I was picked to be a missionary in the Philippines, but my Granddad thought I was too young, and wouldn't let me go.

I left Bible College after a year. I worked in a local fruit shop for six months and met the owner of a care home who suggested I apply for a job with them. Little did I know I'd be a carer for the next 10 years, working with people with dementia and other mental health issues.

M: Was there any love on the horizon?

I met my first husband while I worked at the fruit shop but unfortunately he changed a year after our marriage, and became a control freak. We split up just after my beautiful daughter, Elyssia, was born, but fate is a wonderful thing, and I met my second husband soon after and in an online chat-room of all places. We've just celebrated our 10th wedding anniversary.

M: And now you're a busy mum.

I have four children; the three youngest have autism.

When I first embarked on this journey of autism, I never realised it would change my whole way of thinking, and life as I knew it. I learned not to take anything for granted; learned to think outside the box. You see, the three youngest also have global delay development, hypermobility and gene 16p 11.2 microduplication. Only three people in every ten thousand have Gene 16p 11.2. I have the three children with it, which unfortunately has a knock on effect with our eldest, Elyssia.

Luke, Elyssia, Zak, and Jenna

Elyssia is 13 and your typical teen, full of attitude and teenage angst. She loves One Direction, especially Liam and Louis, and 80s music (It's not down to me listening to it all the time. Honest! LOL)

She sits and reads for hours, and loves the Harry Potter books and films. Her favourite authors are J. K. Rowling and Jacqueline Wilson. She sometimes plays X-box, usually Harry Potter, Minecraft, and likes games on the computer, such at Temple Run, and puzzle solving games.

Despite this, she is unable to be a 'typical' teen because so much consideration has to be given to her three siblings varying complex needs. She is unable to have friends round, and knows we can't go out on the spur of the moment. It takes weeks of planning ahead to go out for the day.

Luke is 8. I didn't realise that there was something wrong with Luke. I thought he was just being stubborn. But when he stopped talking at 18 months, alarm bells started ringing. He lived in a silent world just staring into space for hours, unaware of the world around him. It wasn't until he was three years old, that he received a diagnosis of autism. This opened a whole new world to me.

Jenna is 7. Jenna was a very routine orientated baby. She didn't cope when things went wrong, and would scream for hours on end. Luke and Jenna never slept, and would be awake till 4 a.m., then suddenly go to sleep till 6 a.m. and wake up full of beans.

Zak is 3. I knew as soon as Zak was born that something wasn't right. He likes routine, doesn't sleep, and screams. He had a lot of problems when he was born. He was four weeks premature, and couldn't maintain his body temperature. It was touch and go whether we would both survive as my blood pressure was extremely high, and the medics couldn't control it. They couldn't get Zak warm until they put him skin to skin with me and he soon warmed up.

Zak was diagnosed with autism when he was 18 months old. The specialist that saw Luke when he was first diagnosed also saw Zak, and said that he was worse than Luke was at that age. They all know our family very well.

A couple of years ago Luke and Jen took part in research of Gene 16p 11.2 microduplication. We don't know much about this rare chromosome disorder Gene 16p 11.2 except that 3 people in every 10,000 have it, and it affects the way they take information in, their sleep and eating patterns etc. Because I have three children with this gene, I was curious to know more about it.

I was nervous about meeting the researchers as I wasn't sure how the kids would react because usually they don't like strangers in the house. After a few minutes of meeting the two researchers S and J, all my worries vanished as the kids took a liking to them straight away.

The afternoon was very interesting as we went through a questionnaire that delved into the children's behaviour and personality. It was something I had never sat down and thought about. I have always taken Luke and Jen for who they are, never judging them as society does. It certainly gave me food for thought, and made me see the children's quirks in a different light. It made me realize that Luke and Jen were so unique due to their quirks that this is what separates them from a neurotypical child.

With Luke and Jen it's not about hitting the major achievements and milestones that counts; it's the minor ones. For instance; how Jen is elated every time she writes a new letter. Or the fact that Luke loves the weather and sits for hours just watching the weather channel.

M: Do the children go to a mainstream school, and if so do you feel their needs are being met?

At the moment this is playing a big part in our life. Luke goes to a special school and is doing extremely well due to smaller groups, and one-to-one staff support. Jenna goes mainstream, and is not coping. We have tried to get her statement of educational needs since she was in reception. Her previous school helped as much as possible, working with her in a small group, making social stories etc. She just moved up to middle school, and in an ideal world I would have loved for her to have started at a special school, but without a statement it's not possible.

I realized how much routine controlled Jenna when her school decided they would have an inset day; not at the end of the week, or the start of the week, (which would have been more logical) but right in the middle of the week. When she arrived home from school after the event she was like a caged animal that was suddenly let loose, and there was no calming her. She was screaming, and throwing things, displaying so much more than a tantrum; it was a full blown meltdown. It was so upsetting to see this normally happy, smiley girl snap, and become this whirlwind of torment; uncontrollable, and inconsolable. It took hours for her to calm down and all this because her school routine had been disrupted.

M: How much difference has internet access made to your life?

As the years passed, my passion to learn more about autism/additional needs grew. I knew it wasn't easy to go out, or attend the playgroups, and it soon became very apparent that there wasn't much support for families with children on the spectrum. We have a local group of special needs parents that meet up, but due to transport, and attending appointments I was unable to go.

I started to write a blog about being a parent to children with autism/additional needs. Some days autism, and all its quirks, seem to overwhelm me, and take over my whole being and I feel I can't cope. I noticed putting my feelings down helped me, and at the same time it was supporting others. The response from parents was yes, I know exactly how you feel.

My blog soon became not only a place to write my musings, but support for other parents as well. It also became apparent that people who had never heard about autism were starting to read more about it.

My support, apart from my husband, is online. Through the media of Twitter, Facebook, and blogging, I feel I am not alone.

Coming to terms with having three children with autism, though they are dearly loved, was devastating at first, and what didn't help was watching people I considered friends or acquaintances, withdraw from my life.

I remember standing at the school gates and thinking, *Why don't the other parents talk to me anymore? Why do they stand so far away?*

I saw them in their huddles all chatting away, but they no longer included me in their conversations.

What had changed?

My son Luke used to make funny noises as I waited for my daughter to come out of school. I wasn't sure why he made these noises, but it explained why no one talked to me.

After incidents like that, I can go home, switch on my computer and tell my friends around the world what happened. I'd immediately feel the love, support, and most of all the understanding because many of my internet friends also have children on the spectrum, and have had similar experiences.

M: You've not been well, have you?

I have heard so many times that the human body can only cope with so much. What happens when you reach that point?

How much is too much?

They don't tell you that bit do they? You have to find that out yourself.

124

I had my first stroke in April 2012. Everyone said that things would improve; that I would feel better but it was going to take time. It wasn't until I had my MRI scan on my brain that the full extent of damage the multiple mini strokes or TIA's had caused was known, as it showed part of my brain has died.

I recently had a heart operation to close a hole in my heart that I had since birth. It was only through talking to my Cardiologist consultant that I realised the strokes were caused by this hole in the heart. I can't walk very far as the strokes have robbed me of co-ordination, and have left a significant weakness in my right side. So it has been suggested that I maybe have to think about getting a mobility scooter so I can get out and about. My husband has made adaptions where he can, and has moved the outside decking as I couldn't cope with the step down to the garden. So now I just walk straight on to the decking as it is right next to the door.

M: Do you have much support from the health service?

We have a lovely GP who is so pro-active with the family, and has done so much for us. He has currently referred me to OT and Physio because of my mobility issues. I can't walk very far, manage the stairs, or get into the bath. We live in a housing association town house so when I get this referral they will put in a walk in shower for us. We were lucky to get this house; it was brand new and overlooks the sea. We all love it.

I feel at last people are listening to our pleas when we say we are not coping. We have also been referred for some more help and support; someone who is going to support the *whole* family, not just the children. I hope that as things change, and I claw my life back, that we will continue to go forward and have a good quality of life.

125

I am really looking forward to Christmas as last year was the first time in 7 years we were able to have a Christmas tree. Now for the first time ever we will be able to sit down and enjoy our Christmas meal as a family. Things such as this I never take for granted.

I am trying to get Zak, who has lots of sensory issues when it comes to food, to eat. At the moment he is living on special fortified milk but I want him to start trying new foods and textures. I think if he can sit with us while we are eating that he will join us for Christmas dinner.

M: What are your hopes for the future?

The one thing, and my dearest wish that no money can buy, is for the kids to be accepted for who they are.

No prejudice.

No ignorance.

And that they could lead a perfectly happy life with no worries of how people will react to them.

For them not to get upset and scream when the world around them becomes too much, and they feel over powered.

For people to be more understanding, and not always think the kids are naughty when in fact they aren't, unfortunately they can't help the way they act.

Yes, that's what I want for the future.

I would like to finish my story with a poem my eldest daughter, Elyssia wrote.

Give Autism a Chance

I live with autism each and every day as my 3 siblings all have autism.

People always run, back away, when I or anyone else uses the word AUTISM.

People that have autism in fact have a real gift; they can be intelligent in different topics.

I mean my little brother Luke who is only 8 years old already knows more about computers and aeroplanes, even more than I do or ever will.

My sister Jen is really good at history and can remember and recite facts of history she was told months ago.

Then there is Zak who at 3 years can use an ipad himself and knows what he likes.

Autism means that their brain is wired differently and they see things from another perspective.

But, what people don't realise is that they are the same as you and me. So next time you hear the word autism don't back away. Remember how amazing they are despite the fact that they can't cope in social situations.

Give autism a chance you might learn something from it.

Lesley Chan

"**Amélie** has had 22 trips to theatres, several surgeries, two Nissan fundoplication for reflux disease—first one failed—many aspirations and this has made her lungs chronic, and she has bronchiectasis. Amélie remains oxygen dependent, tracheostomy, gastrostomy, doesn't eat food, but loves to taste food. Amélie has no hearing nerves, so she will never hear sounds or speak, she is partially sighted and requires 24/7 nursing care."

Lesley's Journey

I was born in 1968 in Salford, Manchester, and by the tender age of 18 months I had a heart operation myself, so me and my girl have matching scars, identical yet 38 years apart. Family life was like most those days, two parents, both hard working, mass on Sundays, and back for benediction with Granny Barton at 4 p.m. Caravan holidays to the coast line, and the school holidays were always spent all day, everyday, outside playing cricket and football with my two brothers.

At 15 I met my one and only true love, and now husband, Darren. He was 19, and we met in our local rugby club where my brothers and cousin also played. My father was poorly with cancer, and my mum said Darren was "too old" for me. Of course when your Ma tells you this, like most females, I became a little defiant.

I left school and immediately started work as a dental nurse, qualified at the Manchester Dental Hospital, and then stayed with this profession until Amélie's birth. I was also a Special Constable with the Greater Manchester Police force for 18 months as I thought I wanted to be a police officer.

When I was 17, my father lost his fight with cancer and died aged 42, and this would be the first devastating event in my life. Darren and I moved in together the following year—1986—and have been together ever since. We were married on the island of Jamaica in 1991, and now have four gorgeous daughters.

Gabrielle, is 19 and following Mum's footsteps into nursing. She is a student Paediatric nurse at Edge Hill University.

Olivia, is 17 and our most chilled out child. She's played for Manchester City Ladies Football Club 8 years now, and captained them to win the treble. She adores football, and wants to be a PE teacher. Olivia is currently in her second year at college, and also works behind the bar at the rugby club where Darren and I met 30 years ago :)

Fleur is 10 and is adorable. She has been raised in hospital. When Amélie was born, Fleur was just 14 months old, and the two are inseparable. She is a full time young carer in her own right. She tube feeds Amélie, and suctions her nose, helps with all her cares, and is such a caring girl as a result.

M: Tell us about when Amélie was born.

The birth of our fourth child would be our last. Although we were excited I was also feeling exhausted towards the end of pregnancy. There had been a number of reduced baby movements that I had never experienced with our three other children, and excessive amniotic fluid (polyhydramnios). Following a diabetes test result, I was scanned and reassured by the obstetric team that my baby was "fine" and diagnosed as "gestational diabetic." I have since become wary of the word *fine*!

Amélie Mia entered the world a full term baby and was

131

delivered by elective caesarean section (due to previous caesarean section) on Monday, 10th January, 2005. We eagerly awaited some healthy sounds of crying...they did not arrive, just a very feeble attempt at one. The Midwife provided some facial oxygen and stimulation in what seemed like an eternity, then, very promptly dressed Amélie, and encouraged a first feed in view of gestational diabetes, regardless of Amélie having obvious facial palsy, subtle dysmorphia, absent ear lobe or pinna, low set ears, epicanthus fold, sandal gap toes, and abnormal eyes. Since I have trained and become a midwife, this is the one issue I do have in all of Amélie's care to date; the serious lack of observational skills of the newborn.

M: How did that first feed go?

Amélie was fed, and the milk regurgitated down her nostrils. Darren immediately alerted the midwife, and asked if it was normal. It became quickly evident that this feed had descended Amélie into respiratory depression, although we were reassured all was "fine." *There's that word again!* I was also reassured this is normal for a baby born by caesarean section, and informed promptly Amélie had "wet lung" and things would improve with antibiotics.

M: It was a lot for you to be coping with straight after C-section.

During the immediate days of Amélie's birth I kept com-plaining of chest pain, and having been reviewed several times, doctors reassured me all is "fine" and I was suffering with anxiety because my baby was poorly. I later collapsed on the special care unit, slid to the floor with difficulty catching my breath. My husband described me as blue lips, sweaty, and whiter than white. All was not *fine*. The nurse said she was concerned about me and thank

God a VQ scan was requested.

M: And then Amélie's health further deteriorated?

Whilst I was being assessed, Amélie was now suffering seizures, and heart murmurs were detected. A rapid transfer to a regional unit to be ventilated took place. I was informed I could not transfer with Amélie as I had to wait for my scan and results.

Never separate mums and babies is my only feelings here as this was to be the worst hours of my life, and is something I am very passionate about when I care for families with babies going unexpectedly to the neonatal unit.

The following evening my husband is at Amélie's bedside as she is now fighting for her life; my three daughters are living at my parents' house, and I am alone and being diagnosed with a pulmonary embolism (blood clot on my lung). Following these results the medics rushed in to weigh me, try and get a pair of stockings on my legs, and provide me with 10mg Warfarin and fragmin injection. I prefer to call this *after the event care*, especially as I had told staff several times I was having chest pain and difficulty breathing! Repeatedly distressed by calls made to my heartbroken hubby, I asked to be transferred to the hospital where Amélie was ventilated, again I was told there were no beds at the hospital, so there's only one thing for me to do—sign myself out. Reckless as it sounds, I left in my pyjamas, carrying a yellow booklet for anti-coagulation clinic, and lots of injections and Warfarin—my new best friend—and was presented upon discharge with a white piece of paper to sign myself out. My baby was far more important than my own health, so I left.

Once I had seen Amélie, and realised how critical her situation was, I went home to pack a bag.

I was not leaving my girl again.

M: So, having signed yourself out of hospital, you're running around the house packing an overnight bag; your girls are with their Grandparents, your new baby and hubby are in a neonatal unit, and you've just had a section, and also been diagnosed with a pulmonary embolism. You must have been running on adrenalin.

Unfortunately, the brain kicked in whilst packing, and I quickly Googled pulmonary embolism. It wasn't the wisest move I had ever made. After reading that pulmonary embolism is the leading cause of maternal death, 2005, I rapidly attempted to readmit myself to the hospital I had just discharged from. The A&E staff were sympathetic but could only admit me to a geriatric ward, not a maternity ward.

M: Could things have gotten any worse?

I then made a tearful SOS call to my tearful husband. The neonatal nurse caring for Amélie was very sympathetic, and arranged a bed for me at the same hospital as my baby on the postnatal maternity ward. I promptly left in a taxi and hurried to my husband and baby.

And so the long NICU journey had begun. We welcomed the expert advice from Dr Lydia Bowden, our new Consultant Neonatologist—the most wonderful medical doctor whom we have trusted for the last 8 years. I was irritated by the endless "Are you married to your cousin?" question from junior doctors who were eager to learn what was wrong with my baby. For weeks, other questions followed every shift handover, such as "Have you been ill or exposed to anything in your pregnancy? Do you smoke? Do you drink alcohol?" I was a sensible pregnant mother, and I answered all questions with a *No*. Nonetheless, the culture of blaming myself for Amélie's surgeries, and unknown condition began to take their toll.

M: You searched high and low for a diagnosis?

We could not sleep on the NICU unit, so every night after arriving home late I would enter the Google search tool, and search syndromes and images. All I had to go on was Amélie's abnormally shaped ear, heart defects, and optic nerve colobomas (partially sighted) that had been diagnosed. I asked her team if she had di-george syndrome, and also VCF was in the running. Dr Bowden told us that sometimes children are left without a diagnosis. She encouraged me to stop searching as they were doing all they could to find the missing puzzles to the jigsaw. My girl was a jigsaw; this didn't offend me, but I searched more intensely. Not finding a reason for Amélie's condition became my biggest fear; the not knowing, and endless culture of blame I now placed upon myself.

Three weeks of age and hundreds of syndromes later—all printed out on the conservatory floor in piles of No, Maybe, or Probable—I woke Darren up (not the first time I had done this) at 04.00 a.m. with CHARGE syndrome pictures of the ears of children described like Amélie. Darren replied that I had to stop doing this, we were also leaving at 6:00 a.m. for Alder Hey for surgery, so dismissive of Darren's thoughts and words, I put all the CHARGE syndrome info into my bag.

When Amélie arrived in an ambulance at Alder Hey there were no intensive care beds in the hospital. She was eventually taken by ambulance to her local hospital…possibly the worst ever car journey for Darren and I as we had to travel separately, and when she was delayed arriving back, I entered what I would describe as one of the very many of my meltdowns!

On arrival back to our unit, post heart surgery, I asked my baby's team if she had CHARGE syndrome. The staff were dismissive and said I should speak to Dr Bowman on

Monday morning. It was a long weekend waiting to speak with the doctor, but the more I searched and made internet contact with families abroad, the more I knew Amélie had CHARGE syndrome. Dr Bowman agreed to have the geneticist come see us. A few days later she agreed that our little girl did have some subtle features of CHARGE syndrome. I had by now read further and told her a woman in the Netherlands had found the gene CHD7 on chromosome 8 and could we send Amélies blood to this team. The UK did not test for CHARGE in 2005. Our geneticist, equally as empathetic as Dr Bowden, agreed and also told me Amélie did not have di-george or VCF. Bloods were sent to the Netherlands, and this would be a very long six months to await their analysis; not sure if this was due to back-log from newly diagnosed syndrome finding, or another reason.

In the meantime I put information about CHARGE syndrome at Amélie's incubator, and attempted to explain to NICU nurses how children with the condition couldn't bear the light (full strip light above her incubator), and with multi-sensory impairment featuring high on the syndrome spectrum, could sudden movements when caring for her be the reason she became distressed.

M: How were your suggestions met by the ward staff?

They went down like a lead balloon, and I was now obviously sensing the parent labelled *who does she think she is.* My life on the NICU unit became very difficult from here onwards.

I overheard negative staff comments about me, and it saddened me they should feel this way. In my humble opinion, I was a devastated mummy needing to know why my term baby had been born so sick, especially with three healthy girls at home. My desire was not to irritate staff, but to try and understand my girl's exceptional needs. I have to emphasise that at no point did our Consultant, Dr Bowden, ever make either Darren or I feel this way.

In the weeks that followed, Amélie should have been recovering well following her heart surgery, but she deteriorated further, and a new heart scan revealed Cardiomyopathy, that was not present on the echo prior to surgery. The doctor asked me if I was a diabetic (which by now I was not) but this plummeted me further into the *it's all my fault mode again.*

In April 2005, surgery for a Nissan fundoplication to prevent recurrent aspirations into her lungs was performed, and feeding became easy with the gastrostomy; Amélie currently feeds 12 hours a day now.

At 6 months of age, our geneticist confirmed CHARGE syndrome. At long last we could truly learn how best to help our girl, ensure care and education meets her individualised needs, and advocate for her effectively.

M: What's it like being a midwife and how many babies do you think you've helped bring into this world?

Being a midwife is incredibly challenging, especially with so many small units closing, increased birth rates, and a national shortage of midwives.

People's expectations are much higher than years ago, even so, I feel we have an NHS to be proud of...although it's wearing me out with long shifts!! There are some very special families I meet and never forget; amazing outcomes, and some in grief, I feel I have a lot to offer the ones that are sad, maybe that's my experience of Amélie's birth, not having any special happy memories. Mostly I prefer not to remember the early years. I've delivered lots of babies as I work on the birth centre, but I've no idea how many, possibly a couple of hundred by now.

M: You've obviously been a great advocate over the years, and one of the biggest fights was for Amélie's right to a decent education. Sadly for most parents transition from one stage of specialised schooling to the next is no longer an automatic rite of passage. How have you navigated your way around the education system, and is it meeting Amélie's needs?

Amélie was placed in the early year's education setting at a local education school for special needs children. Initially, we were told how she would struggle to learn, multi-

sensory impaired and clearly neurologically abnormal according to the neurologist, Darren and I happily agreed we didn't need to see her again for input...too negative!

As we began to realise Amélie was trying to learn, we became in contact with a teacher of the deaf, but Amélie was only provided with one hour per week at school. Our TOD said Amélie had potential with the useful vision she had to be able to learn sign language. The special needs teachers disagreed and said that sign-a-long was a sufficient language to learn. Sign-a-long supports hearing children and Amélie has no hearing nerves. Darren asked at one parents evening if they felt she would improve surrounded by deaf peers, they disagreed and said "she was hardly the brightest child in the class" Darren replied "can the other children hear?" Of course they could, and this fleeting statement set my mind a blaze.

I contacted the nearest school for the DEAF, but they declined saying Amélie was too medicalised at this age, but they would re-visit her health. Our bigger challenge was the LEA who had a psychologist review Amélie, and said "no" to any such move out of the authority. She felt the school was meeting *all* Amélie's needs. Of course I refuted this statement, challenged it as a basic human right to an education in a language a deaf child could benefit from.

We never gave up with this, and 2 years on the school revisited Amélie and agreed they could accept her, but the LEA declined the move. So I went on my "momonamission" mode. I emailed, wrote, and corresponded to anyone who would listen, reply, and evaluate. We eventually won our appeal.

What saddens me most is what about those families where parents don't have that fight left in them? What happens to children where the LEA says no, and this is not challenged?

Amélie has excellent sign language, and communicates all her needs as a result of her wonderful school for the DEAF—Thomasson Memorial, in Bolton. Our next challenge will be age 11, and where she will go from there? More challenges ahead…sigh…why must it be like this?

M: Do you have any respite support?

We frequent Derian House Hospice when we can. My girls have grown up sleeping in the hospice, playing with disabled kids as we never leave Amélie alone. She can't speak or communicate unless the other person has BSL (British Sign Language) and sadly, no-one does use sign language, so leaving her is not, and never will be, an option.

M: So the girls stay with Amélie at the hospice so you and Dad can have a break? That's so nice...

Yes. I have to say, having been left with my parents a lot, and to their own devices as we slept in hospital mostly for the first three years of Amélie's life, we are so very proud of how beautiful and caring each girl is...and has turned out.

Life for them has been very difficult, they miss holidays abroad that we enjoyed before Amélie's birth, and a lifestyle that we no longer have. They've never resented it or her. Amélie is pivitol to each sister, and her cares are always their priorities. Hugely proud of them !

M: And today, you're still packing that overnight bag for hospital?

16th December 2005, was her biggest fight for her life, following a severe pulmonary arrest, Amélie was resuscitated using intra-osseous resuscitation following post RSV+ Bronchiolitis. When a child survives this, you know they're resilient, and meant to survive regardless of the odds.

Amélie spent four months in NICU. A brief homecoming followed but for the next 2 years she was mostly hospitalised. Amélie has had 22 trips to theatres, several surgeries, two surgeries for Nissan fundoplication for reflux disease—first one failed—many aspirations which have made her lungs chronic, she has bronchiectasis. Amélie remains oxygen dependent, tracheostomy, gastrostomy, doesn't eat food, but loves to taste food. Amélie has no hearing nerves so she will never hear sounds or speak; she is partially sighted, and requires 24/7 nursing care.

Amélie has absent semi-circular canals so she finally walked aged 5 years 6 months, although she does have serious issues with balance, and her deaf blindness.

Darren gave up work to care for Amélie, and in view of life changing events, and financial commitments—mortgage etc., I retrained to become a Midwife based on a single statement of "God only sends special children to special parents." I studied, and slept, at my little girl's hospital bedside whilst she was intubated. Darren went home at night to see our girls (guilt and neglectful sibling thoughts haunt me.)

I somehow managed a one-to-one class honours degree and award for Student midwife of the year 2009.

I now work full-time, and bank shift every week, and most of my annual leave, to bring home the finances for two.

Winter I despise you. In September, November, and December 2013—3 admissions already this winter with chest infection.

We have many hospital consultants and appointments, daily growth hormones injections continue, and I provide Amélie intravenous antibiotics into her central line at home every three months and when poorly. Occasionally—when her bloods are seriously abnormal—she has to stay in hospital for couple of days!

We are eternally grateful, and indebted to all the amazing professionals helping my girl along the way. You are the unsung heroes of the NHS.

Our lives changed forever the day Amélie was born. I have since come to realise there are no regrets of having our beautiful girl, but there has become a whole host of nursing skills to be learnt; responsibility no parent should have to endure. Countless campaigns for what her individual needs are, and sleep deprivation beyond that of any newborn child…in fact nine years on and the sleep deprivation has continued with an expected four hours sleep that has become our norm. We don't want pity—our love is unconditional. Amélie lights up our home with her personality like no other…such a unique, rare, and beautiful child. Our ethos in life is; Amélie must have inclusion at every possible level.

Amélie

A precious gift from God above
As man and wife, made from much love
We anxiously waited for your imminent date
Hoping and praying you would not be too late

All systems in place and ready to go
Hoping your birth would not be too slow
Excitement and fear, emotions are high
Labour pain arrives, and there's lots of sighs

A glimpse of you, it's all worth the strain
Although our joy turns quickly to pain
Your first day of life, unable to hold
Our unique bond, I feared they stole

Your tiny lungs they made no sound
Your beating heart could not be found
Anxiety inside me started to grow
Tears welled in my eyes, then into a flow

You're snatched away to another place
I can't hide the grief, etched on my face
Doctors baffled, no answers can they find
Machines and wires, I am out of my mind

A devastating time, hurting deep within
Did I do something wrong?
Maybe a sin?

My heart is aching to hold you tight
But it's difficult to see any glimmer of light
Your pain and suffering, I'm feeling so low
But I sense from you a refusal to go

All the pain you are feeling, I feel it too
And if I could make one wish
Then it would be to fix you
You have battled this long
You must never give in
You have to remain strong

And no…there was never a sin

For I realise now, how lucky we are
To have such an amazing child
Most definitely a star
Our precious Amélie always touching lives
Our wonderful daughter, despite odds, still alive…

Jane Raca was invited to talk about her son James, and her campaign to improve social care provision under the Children and Families Bill.

Jane Raca

I was born in the Midlands in the 1960's and had an ordinary, uneventful childhood. Then my parents separated when I was 12, and my father emigrated to the US when I was 15. My mother, who had been a housewife, went back to work as a secretary to support my sister and me. She had a strong belief in education, and encouraged me to study hard. With her help I ended up at Bristol University, where I read law. That's where I met my husband, Andrew.

Once we graduated, we started working in London. Andrew was very involved in Tory politics, and since it was the 1980's there were lots of dinners, and conferences with famous people. It felt glamorous and privileged. By the late 1990's I was a partner in a national law firm, and had my first child, Tom. We lived in a nice house, and life seemed as good as it gets. Then James, our second son, was born 15 weeks early with severe brain damage. He has cerebral palsy, epilepsy, severe learning disabilities, and severe autism. He can't walk, or talk, or use his left hand.

The journey we went through after his birth was so profound, and the fight to get help for him so difficult, that after 10 years I felt compelled to write a book about it. *Standing up for James* was published in 2012. It received some media coverage, and I was amazed by the emails I got afterwards from people who, like me, had had to battle for everything they needed. Since then, I have campaigned for better support for disabled children; particularly respite, and help at home for parents caring 24/7. Some parents have been so desperate through lack of sleep and a proper break from their responsibilities, that they have taken their own lives. I thought about doing that in my darkest moments.

When the government announced that it was introducing a bill to improve the system for disabled children, I was relieved, but worried that it didn't go far enough to improve social care provision. I wrote to the Prime Minister about the gaps in the Children and Families Bill, and asked parents to email him in support. (You can read the letter at the end of this story.) Many children's charities also lobbied the government, including Mencap, the National Autistic Society, Scope, Every Disabled Child Matters campaign, and the Council for Disabled Children. At the eleventh hour, we had a partial victory. The government agreed to a pilot scheme to look into making it easier for parents to appeal against local authorities if they weren't getting the social care they needed.

The Children and Families Bill will become law in late 2014, and the pilot scheme may run for up to 3 years after that. We don't know whether the pilot will lead to the changes which need to happen. However, I am committed to continuing the campaign to make them a reality.

As for coming to terms emotionally with having a disabled child, I can best describe it by quoting an article I wrote for SEN magazine in March 2013.

In the summer of 1999, I was sitting on Whitby beach with my husband and our 2 year old toddler. There was a strong breeze which kept blowing sand into our ice creams, but the sky was bright blue, and the sun danced on the surface of the sea.

I didn't know that the next day would bring a tsunami with it, one that would destroy the life I knew, and leave me to rebuild a completely different one. I was only 24 weeks pregnant and my waters broke. Three days later James was born, weighing just 1lb 12oz, with extensive brain damage. The doctors told us that he only had a 50 per cent chance of surviving. If he did live, he would at the very least have movement difficulties down one side. He might be much

worse; they couldn't say.

My memories of those first weeks and months are hazy, as all my experiences were clouded by shock. There were the times that James nearly died in hospital; then, when he finally pulled through, a sense of blazing joy. This was followed by his homecoming, and the terrifying responsibility of nursing him myself.

Gradually, the shock subsided, to be replaced by the day-to-day realities of James's condition. At first, he looked like any other baby. No new-born can walk or talk, and James was handsome and smiley, so we did not have to deal with difficult questions. Then, as other children began to reach their milestones and he didn't, he began to get left behind, like seaweed on the beach when the tide goes out.

The process was so gentle—almost imperceptible—that most of the time I just enjoyed having my baby and was happy that he was alive. Even when he was diagnosed with cerebral palsy, I was alright and felt safe in the little bubble of our own home. But when I went out into the wider world, things began to happen which pierced that bubble.

On the first occasion, I was in a jewellery shop getting a watch repaired, and James was in his pushchair. The shop was empty and the woman serving me had plenty of time to look at him. I saw that he had his left hand up in a classic spastic pose. "He's got cerebral palsy" I said, and the woman smiled kindly and said she knew. It was the first time I had spoken the words to anyone, and the pain of hearing that sentence through my own mouth was intense. After that, I began to tell everyone, rather than wait to be asked. Each time it became a little easier, like a wound which had bled, but was now healing, and was thick with scar tissue.

Eventually it became clear that James couldn't walk, and since he was too big for his pushchair, he would have to graduate to a wheelchair. Having a blue badge and a wheelchair defined James as a physically disabled person, in a way that a diagnosis, invisible from the outside, did not.

The next piercing of our bubble came with the special school. I had never been to one, or known anyone who had been to one. Special schools were invisible parts of our society, rarely talked about and usually hidden away. Suddenly there was a nursery full of children like James. Seeing him in context took my breath away.

Once the special school became involved with us, the labels defining James's disability increased in number. We became familiar with the language of therapy and special education: profound and multiple learning difficulties

148

(PMLD), speech and language therapists (SaLTs), and occupational therapists (OTs). The SaLT taught James to use pictures to communicate, and it confirmed what I had long suspected; that although he couldn't speak, he knew exactly what was going on.

We learned that James's right to be at the special school depended on him having a statement of SEN. This was a piece of paper which I had put away without even reading. I didn't know then that some parents have to fight to get a statement, and that it was to become very important later in James's life.

James had a couple of seizures which the doctors had classified as febrile—temperature related—because he had been ill. The school nurses sent home a form headed "THIS CHILD IS EPILEPTIC" for us to fill in. He hadn't been diagnosed as epileptic though, and I was hoping, seriously hoping, that he wasn't. I didn't want James to face a lifetime of medication and hospitals. I took my fear and emotion out on the head teacher, complaining bitterly about the form, which was hastily withdrawn.

Months later, when James had nearly suffocated in the night during a series of fits, I was only too glad when he was prescribed epilepsy medicine and issued with emergency sedatives. The form was quietly reinstated at school, and I helped to fill it in.

The last stab, which deflated our bubble completely, arrived out of the blue. James had some unusual behaviour which I had just dismissed as "James".

He didn't like going out in the car, wouldn't eat warm food, and retched when he saw anything bright orange. His nursery teacher sat me down and said she thought he might be autistic. By this stage my feelings had become numb, and hearing this caused only a dull ache. When the diagnosis was confirmed by his consultant, I realised that at some level I had known about the autism, yet as with the cerebral palsy and the epilepsy, I had wanted not to know. Now, in addition to the wheelchair and the anti-fitting medication, we had to adapt our family life for a member who was terrified by change of routine, and needed constant support to cope with the world around him.

It has taken 13 years to be able to say, without any lump in my throat, "My son has cerebral palsy and epilepsy and is severely autistic. He uses a wheelchair, and can't walk or talk." This acceptance has no doubt happened with the passage of time, but it has also come about because these conditions are part of James and I love all that he is.

The tsunami, that washed away the world I knew, took with it my prejudice and preconceptions. I am no longer scared by seeing someone who can't speak words making unusual sounds. I no longer get embarrassed by meeting people with a learning disability. I am not interested in how someone dresses or whether they live in the right part of town. Having James has taught me instead to look for the humanity within.

Letter to Rt Hon David Cameron MP

9 December 2013

Dear Prime Minister...

I am the mother of a severely disabled child. He has cerebral palsy, epilepsy, learning disabilities, challenging behaviour, and is severely autistic. He uses a wheelchair, can't walk or talk, can't use his left hand and is doubly incontinent. I am writing to you to express my concern over the lack of social care provision for children like him.

151

Many local authorities are failing to provide respite and home carers, and this is causing great suffering. There are parents trying to survive for years, raising their children on little sleep, with no breaks and no help. They are experiencing depression, exhaustion and marital breakdown. They have no hope of affording the ongoing specialist care which is needed.

If they can summon the strength to take on their local social care department, they face a lengthy, ineffectual complaints process. What they need is a fast, independent forum, with the power to award the necessary support for their child.

The children and families' bill misses a golden opportunity to achieve this. It introduces joint education, health and care (EHC) plans in place of statements of special educational needs. For the first time parents will have all their disabled child's needs recorded in one place. But they will still only be able to appeal the education content of the plans to an independent tribunal, as is the case now. That happened to my family; we won an appeal over my son's school, but it took us another five years to get the social care he needed. Why can't the bill provide a right of appeal to tribunal, over all the contents of EHC plans?

The government has said that it doesn't support a right of appeal against social care issues. It doesn't want local authorities to be under a statutory duty to provide the care part of individual EHC plans, since they may not have enough money to look after both disabled children and children at risk.

This is the finite resources argument, and goes to the heart of the matter. We define ourselves as a society by the priorities we choose. Surely these priorities include providing humane levels of support to people who from birth will never be able walk or talk, let alone work? This should not have to be at the expense of protecting children at risk of abuse. Pitching those two sets of critical needs against each other is unacceptable.

The National Autistic Society has presented the government with a petition of over 10,000 signatures on the importance of a single point of appeal from all parts of EHC plans. That is a lot of parents, but it is also just the tip of the iceberg.

They are telling you that they are not prepared to carry on bat-tling on all sides. They need the EHC plans to make a real difference to the most vulnerable people in our society.

Yours sincerely

Jane Raca

We hope you've enjoyed *Warrior Mums*. These stories, along with more family photos, can be found on my blog: http://www.michelledaly.blogspot.com

If you'd like to be featured in the next Warrior Mum series, please contact me at: michelleannedaly@yahoo.co.uk.

6275197R00099

Printed in Great Britain
by Amazon.co.uk, Ltd.,
Marston Gate.